The Truth Behind the Rock

The Truth Behind the Rock

An Honest Look at the Myth of the Fairy-Tale Engagement

Jessica Kaminsky

SIMON SPOTLIGHT ENTERTAINMENT
New York   London   Toronto   Sydney

SSE

SIMON SPOTLIGHT ENTERTAINMENT
An imprint of Simon & Schuster
1230 Avenue of the Americas, New York, New York 10020
Also available in a Simon Spotlight Entertainment hardcover edition.
SIMON SPOTLIGHT ENTERTAINMENT and related logo are
trademarks of Simon & Schuster, Inc.
Manufactured in the United States of America
First Edition 10 9 8 7 6 5 4 3 2 1
Library of Congress Cataloging-in-Publication Data
Kaminsky, Jessica.
The truth behind the rock / by Jessica Kaminsky.—1st ed.
p. cm.
ISBN-13: 978-1-4169-1142-5 (hc)
ISBN-10: 1-4169-1142-1 (hc)
[1. Man-woman relationships. 2. Dating (Social customs).
3. Marriage.] I. Title.
HQ801.K327 2006
306.73'4—dc22
2006000174
ISBN-13: 978-1-4169-3358-8 (pbk)
ISBN-10: 1-4169-3358-1 (pbk)

For my parents, Howard and Susan,
who are still making it work after thirty-six years . . .
without ever having gotten engaged

CONTENTS

PREFACE

LET'S GET SOMETHING STRAIGHT. THIS IS NOT A book about how to get a man. Or how to keep a man. Or how to please a man. This is also not some crusty, outdated self-help book your mother buys in the hopes that one day you'll bring home that perfect somebody (or anybody, for that matter). But most important, this book is not *The Rules*. Remember that mid-nineties literary treasure, responsible for such kernels of wisdom as "never accept a date for Friday after Wednesday" and "always let him call you"? Ah, those were some empowering times indeed.

So now that we have that out of the way, let me be the first to assure you that *The Truth Behind the Rock* is the opposite kind of book from what you're probably used to. It isn't going to tell you how to do things differently or mock your pain as you wait and wonder when your guy is going to get off his ass and propose. *The Truth Behind the Rock* will give women a peek behind the curtain at what real couples go through on the road to engagement. You'll hear stories from both sexes about that uncomfortable, hazy time between wanting to be married and actually getting engaged, as well as every scenario in between. So rest assured this book has a little something for everybody.

Now for the backstory: I got the idea for *The Truth Behind the Rock* after a recent visit home. I was catching up with an old friend who was lamenting that she wanted to get engaged to her boyfriend but didn't think they were even remotely close. As far as she could tell, he seemed more than content to keep things the way they were (i.e., frequent overnights, a toothbrush at her place, and the comfort of knowing that he would get laid on his birthday). In fact, she couldn't imagine her guy taking the initiative to bring their relationship to the next level, buying a ring, and surprising her "like the way your husband surprised you," my friend said. Whoa, whoa, whoa. Hang on there, sister. Are we talking about my husband? Was she kidding? Didn't she know that our engagement took two years of gut-wrenching, heart-baring, soul-crushing conversations?

And that it was the culmination of many Camp David summit–like meetings wherein I had to endure such flimflam excuses as "I'm not sure I even believe in marriage" and—after five years of dating, mind you—"What's the rush, anyway?"

After I shared the history of our less-than-storybook engagement with my friend, she was genuinely surprised. All she had heard about was that Hallmark moment when my then-boyfriend Dave got down on bended knee in Central Park in front of a homeless man and a Puerto Rican couple and asked if I would marry him. She had no idea that there had been heated discussions, ultimatums, and not-so-subtle hints. Like the time I tore a Tiffany ad from a magazine and stuck it in his wallet.

I know what you're thinking. And you're right. I had become *that* girl. It was embarrassing. I'm not proud of it. But I didn't know what else to do. I was desperate. And desperate times called for desperate measures. Which is why I would have benefitted tremendously from knowing that I wasn't the first woman to freak out, act irrationally, and become a walking cliché. And yet, somehow in my mind I felt like everyone else out there was having these fairy-tale engagements while I was holding Dave's feet to

THE TRUTH BEHIND THE ROCK

the fire. But after I spoke to some of my other girl-friends, I realized I wasn't alone.

And so, when my friend started to share her frustration over her boyfriend's lack of enthusiasm, it dawned on me: This was an epidemic, and yet no one was talking about it. So many women out there are hoping and waiting for that out-of-the-blue, ring-in-the—Cracker Jack box, violin-serenading, surprise engagement from their boyfriends. But the reality is that this type of engagement story virtually doesn't exist. Of course there are the exceptions. But for the most part, the path to marriage is one fraught with stalemates, tension, and tears. Even more alarming is that this desire for an unprompted, romantic proposal runs against who these women fundamentally are: modern, career-driven, independent. And yet, there is something so old-fashioned about wanting to be proposed to, wanting to be wanted.

This book explores that paradox and seeks to give all women an opportunity to examine other engagements, as well as to reassure them that there is no one way to pop the question. So take comfort in knowing that you are not the only one with a well-meaning, clueless boyfriend. And read on to discover the truth behind the rock.

PART ONE:
BEFORE THE ROCK

1

THE MYTH OF THE ROCK

WHEN PEOPLE TALK ABOUT GETTING ENGAGED, they tend to leave out all the prodding, pushing, nudging, and mental anguish leading up to that monumental day. Why, you might ask? Probably because these aren't really what we'd call "Hallmark moments." And those angst-ridden, tension-filled pre-engagement stories aren't usually the ones that you're dying to run out and gush about to your closest friends. Now I might be going out on a limb here, but I'm guessing you probably feel that those heated debates, screaming fights, and tearful conversations don't shed the best light on the relationship. After all, doesn't tradition dictate that your mate should come to the decision to propose on his own? And if he hasn't been champing at the bit to get engaged, well then, there must be something inherently wrong with you and your relationship, right? No, that's wrong! So breathe a sigh of relief.

This misconception—the one that says he will propose unassisted by the urgings of a fed-up girlfriend—is perpetuated among women, primarily because no one is eager to share the whole story. The truth is people don't discuss their pre-engagement tales of woe because they tend not to be sexy, and rarely are they romantic.

Take it from me. I dated my husband for five years before we got engaged. And for three of those years, I never thought about marriage. Well, maybe a little. I am a girl, after all. But it didn't dominate my world. I didn't go to sleep dreaming of sparkly diamonds, wedding dresses, and first dances. No way. I was just content to be part of a happy, healthy, non-shouting, no-name-calling relationship. And so, there we were, Dave and I, blissfully plodding along in our relatively stress-free four-year-old relationship when I started a new job.

Now, the only reason I bring up the job is because it was there that I first experienced that horrible relationship scrutiny that sometimes occurs among people who barely know each other and are in desperate need of common ground for conversation. So, the state of my relationship became that platform for communication.

The line of questioning began innocently enough.

"What's your boyfriend's name?"

"Dave."

"How long have you been together?"

"Four years."

Then the questions became more probing.

"Are you living together?"

"Not yet."

"What does he do for a living?"

"He's a film editor."

The interview continued until one of my coworkers posed the question: "So . . . if he has a good job, and he claims to love you, why don't you have a ring on your finger?"

Really, my answer should have been, "How dare you presume to know anything about my relationship? Oh, and by the way, mind your own damn business." But instead, I laughed and deflected the question, saying, "It isn't a big deal. We're just not ready yet."

However, later when I arrived home, I found

myself wondering why we weren't there yet. Should I be worried that my boyfriend of four years hasn't proposed? Is there something wrong with him . . . or worse, with me? Why don't I have a big diamond ring on my finger like Brian-in-accounting's wife? And just like that, the seeds of doubt and discontent had been planted by a band of office nerds.

While I'm not proud of the fact that I let my coworkers get to me, at the root of the matter was the complicated concern that plagues so many women—where is my relationship headed? Are we destined to spend the rest of our lives shuttling back and forth from one studio apartment to another, a small suitcase of amenities forever in tow? I know that, in the wake of my coworkers' questions, I couldn't help but wonder if we shared the same vision for our future—a future that involved a wedding, a house, and maybe a baby? I had always assumed we did. But the truth was, we had never discussed it beyond playful pillow talk and late-night musing over what we would name our kid. (Yes to Phoebe and a big no to Joe.) So there I was, my mind suddenly swirling with questions. Did Dave want to get married? If so, to me? And if he did want to get married to me, well then, why wasn't he sweeping me off my

9

feet with a blue Tiffany box the way it's done in the movies? And why, why, why did I have to be the one to set the wheels in motion? While I wasn't any closer to knowing the answers to those questions, it occurred to me that if we were ever to get to the bottom of this issue, we were going to need to talk about our feelings on the subject of (gulp) marriage.

So alas, that's how the marriage issue was first introduced into our relationship. Eventually, I mellowed out and stopped being so suggestible. But it wouldn't be long before I found myself once again wondering, *Why is everyone getting engaged except me?*

Other women seemed to have these amazing stories of being surprised by the perfect princess-cut diamond. They'd go to dinner only to discover their boyfriends had been conspiring with the waiter, who was busy in the kitchen burying the ring in the bottom of a pot of crème brûlée. What the hell! Who were these men? And why didn't I have one of them? And even if Dave did intend to surprise me with a ring, how would he know what I liked? I didn't even know what I liked. As far as I could tell, we were already screwed.

Later, after confiding in a friend that I feared I may

have a defective boyfriend (or even worse, that I might be defective—i.e., not marriage material), I realized I was not alone. Turns out, I knew many women who had been the ones to first broach the subject of marriage. Women who were tired of waiting in the wings for this mythical, perfect, cloud-parting engagement to occur. Why, they wondered, is it only acceptable for the man to bring up his desire to get married? There are two people in each relationship, after all.

And yet, women are still loath to share these kinds of stories with one another. Like my friend Julia—her engagement was perfect on paper (romantic dinner at a tucked-away hotel, diamond ring presented artfully between dinner and dessert, followed by a beautiful night in a luxury suite), but what she hadn't shared were the painful discussions, the ultimatums, and the near breakup it took to get there. So there it was—the proof. A thoughtful, inspired proposal was only half of the truth. In other words, you can't judge a beautiful engagement by its cover story.

So why are women so tight-lipped about the events leading up to their engagement? And why must the idea of the fairy-tale proposal be perpetuated?

Wouldn't we all benefit from knowing what other women have gone through? Life is complicated enough. So let's end the secrecy, I say. It's time to start sharing those awkward exchanges. Because I can promise you, you are not alone.

SOME ENGAGING HISTORY

＊ In the olden days, a chivalrous gentleman would send a pair of gloves to a woman whom he hoped to marry. If she wore the gloves to church on Sunday, it signaled her acceptance of his proposal.

＊ The reason engagement rings are worn on the third finger of the left hand dates back to the early Egyptian belief that the vein of love (*vena amoris*) ran directly from the heart to the top of the third finger on the left hand.

＊ The first recorded diamond engagement ring was given to Mary of Burgundy in 1477 by the Archduke Maximilian I, emperor of Austria.

Jessica Kaminsky

Straight from the Horse's Mouth

Since we've all probably wished at one time or another that we knew what our boyfriends were thinking, I turned to a married guy for his take on that hazy, sometimes confusing, often argument-laden time in his life before he and his lady got engaged. Here's what Mark had to say:

Were you surprised when your girlfriend first brought up the subject of marriage?

No. A few of our friends had recently gotten engaged, so engagements were in the air, so to speak. And I could tell that the subject was weighing heavily on her mind. But what was tough was that, clearly, she had been stewing for so long that when she finally brought up the topic for discussion, there was no right way to react without her becoming totally upset. She was blaming me for "acting" surprised, but we were talking about marriage for the first time. Looking back, I wish there had been more of a dialogue between us earlier. I wanted her to be happy, and clearly the idea of getting engaged was causing her tremendous angst. But she had

shielded me from what was going on inside her head
and was taking her frustration out on me. It wasn't fair.

He Said/She Said

Real-life couples share what brought them together
and made their relationships work.

Sam & Betsy

They met in the spring of 1998 and dated for five
years. This is their story.

ACT ONE
That Gooey, Chewy, Don't-Sleep, Don't-Eat Phase

He said: When Sam first met Betsy he knew right
away (the first night, in fact) that Betsy was the woman
for him. Not only was he smitten by her beauty, but she
was funny, athletic, and could name all one hundred
senators by state and party affiliation. Not to mention,
they had all these bizarre things in common. They had
scars in the same places. They had gone to the same
sleepaway camp (different years). And they were both
from New Jersey. Not two days before, Sam had been

lamenting to a friend that he wished he could meet a quality girl from New Jersey. And then forty-eight hours later, Betsy came along.

She said: Betsy, on the other hand, liked Sam but found herself plagued with uncertainty. Who was this guy who thought he was her soul mate? And who cared that they were both from New Jersey? So were eight million other people. It felt like a bad pickup line. But there was something oddly charming about this foolish romantic, and over time she found herself falling in love.

ACT TWO
Settling In

After the honeymoon phase comes to a close, couples often experience newfound feelings of comfort and security. So what if their days of late-night boozing have ended? At least now they know they're getting laid on a Saturday, a Monday, and a Wednesday. Or maybe just a Monday. Sure their days of sex with relative strangers is over, but couples take a certain satisfaction in knowing that they're reaching a new level, a deeper level, a level that is based on mutual respect and commitment.

He said: Sam summed it up in these terms: "Men are natural hunters. They're always looking for the right woman, the perfect woman. So when that moment of actually deciding to settle down with someone happens, there is a tremendous sense of relief."

She said: Betsy saw Sam's willingness to settle down in another light. As far as she was concerned, men aren't hunters. They're too lazy to hunt. They'd rather hang out on the couch and play video games. After all, meeting someone takes work. First off, you have to leave the house. And then you have to conjure up enough witty banter to engage someone in conversation long enough to pique their interest.

Clearly, Sam did all of those things at least once. How else did he manage to snag a babe like Betsy? That said, given the amount of effort he would need to put into meeting someone else, she was pretty confident that he wasn't going anywhere.

BOTTOM LINE

Sure, Betsy and Sam had their share of arguments, several storm-outs, and a few pieces of damaged furniture that got caught in the crossfire of one of their blowouts. But they were committed to each other and were determined to work out their differences. Besides, Sam reasoned, how could they break up? They had matching moles on their left shoulders.

ACT THREE

Now or Never

Soon several of their close friends started getting engaged, then married. And it seemed like almost every weekend was spent traveling to some quaint Vermont town to witness a pair of late twenty-somethings pledge their undying love and commitment. Marriages were happening all around them, which inevitably raised questions about their own relationship. Specifically, were they heading toward marriage? If so, when?

And as if the pressure they felt on their own was not enough, at almost every wedding someone would inevitably turn to Betsy and Sam and say something like, "You guys are next." And, "When's the big day?" (By the way, if you are one of *those* people, ease up with the questions. You sound like your pushy aunt. And you know what people say about her.) Not surprisingly, Sam and Betsy soon found themselves dreading weddings. The ceremonies started to make Betsy feel uncomfortable and exposed, while Sam dreaded the inevitable argument that would follow.

She said: Whenever someone asked Betsy a wedding-related question, she found herself wanting to scream, "Does it look like I have a ring on my finger? Why don't you go ask Sam when we're getting engaged . . . and let me know what you find out."

It wasn't that getting married was so important to her. She could wait. But she found herself needing to know that Sam also envisioned a future with her, and was committed to taking their relationship to the next level. She wanted to get engaged. So as time went on and still there was no ring, Betsy grew frustrated. She started to look at what he was spending his money on—trips to Vegas, fancy dinners, a new television. He wasn't saving for a ring. He wasn't thinking ahead. He wasn't serious about starting a family.

Of course, she shared none of this with him. Instead she dropped hints. She artfully laid out magazines, conveniently flipped open to De Beers's "a diamond is forever" ads. She also began to casually work non sequiturs into conversation, such as, "You know me, I just love a classic Tiffany setting." Trying to get Sam to propose was becoming a full-time job, and it was exhausting her. She found herself starting to feel resentful, and she let the feeling fester as she stewed. Until one day, she burst.

He said: For Sam, marriage meant trust. And although he knew he could trust Betsy, he felt that she had put up barriers that kept her from trusting him completely. She wanted to get married and yet she was suspicious of him when he wanted to borrow money to pay off his credit card. Who did she think he was? Some oily road-side salesman looking to rip her off with a pyramid scheme? If they were hoping to build a future together, she needed to trust him 100 percent.

And if she didn't trust him, why would she want to marry him? He feared her reasons for wanting to get engaged had more to do with having an answer to the prying questions of smug married people than it had to do with him. So they went to couples' therapy.

THE VERDICT

Both Betsy and Sam had very real fears surrounding the idea of marriage. Betsy didn't want to be alone.

Her parents had divorced when she was very young, and she didn't want to end up on her own like her mom. Sam's hesitation stemmed from the fact that he didn't want to end up in a loveless marriage like his parents. But personal issues aside, they still loved each other and knew they wanted to spend the rest of their lives together. So over Christmas vacation, Sam proposed to Betsy with a vintage Tiffany ring. (See, he had been listening.) They were married nine months later.

Rock Talk: Let's Break It Down

* They are called storybook engagements for a reason—they only exist in fiction, not in real life.

* Remember, there is always a backstory to the official cover story.

* Don't be afraid to put the wind in his sails. If you're waiting for him to come about, you will probably be waiting a very long time.

Jessica Kaminsky

* Opinions—everyone's got them. Just because someone feels compelled to comment on the if, when, and how you should get married doesn't mean you have to listen to them. Follow your inner compass. You are the best judge of what feels right.

* Share your feelings. Don't hold them in until you burst like the Hulk. Whatever you're thinking or feeling, there is a basis for it, so don't be afraid to ask for what you want.

* Give yourself a mantra (try, for instance, "I am not on a schedule"). And remember to listen to it.

* Just as being in a relationship takes work, so too does getting engaged.

* Guys can be dense when it comes to the subject of marriage. But it doesn't mean he doesn't love you or that there is anything wrong with you. He just may need a nudge. Or two. Or three.

* Finally, remember you're with this person for a reason. That's right, you love the clueless moron.

REACHING FOR THE ROCK

I WILL NOT LIE—THIS IS TOUGH. IT'S HARD TO BE the one to bring up the subject of marriage because in doing so you're exposing yourself. When you say, "I hope you envision a future with me the way I do with you," you're showing your soft underbelly. And since you never know for sure what your partner's response is going to be, you are at your most vulnerable.

No matter how well you know your man, you just can't predict what he will say when the topic of spending the rest of your lives together is first broached. And more often than not, you probably won't get the answer you were hoping for and will have to check your reaction. Perhaps you were expecting something more along the lines of, "You want to get married? Me too!" Or, "You read my mind. In fact, I have the ring right here." But instead you got some nervous coughing, a case of flop sweat, and a sudden aversion to eye contact.

And to top it off, it's left up to you to sort through all of those raw emotions without getting too offended and upset. Because while your boyfriend's noncommittal response may feel like a punch in the stomach, oftentimes it's just his knee-jerk, nervous, freaky, "I don't want to end up like my parents" reaction. It may take Herculean strength, but it's your mission not to be offended by his underwhelming response.

Now, your first instinct may be to grab an object and hurl it at his head. Can't he see what a prize you are? Why is he being so resistant? But before you resort to violence, remember that it may hurt your argument as to why you two were meant to spend your lives together.

Of course, all of this is made doubly difficult by the misconception that you are the only woman who has ever had to be the first to raise the topic of marriage. The fact is, many women initiate conversations regarding the status of their relationship. And yet

THE TRUTH BEHIND THE ROCK

women act as if they've never had these conversations with their future husbands. (How unladylike. It just isn't done!) Consequently, everyone goes around pretending. "I was minding my own business when, all of a sudden, my boyfriend swept me off my feet and whisked me away to a fabulous dinner where a two-carat princess-cut canary diamond was presented on bended knee while we were serenaded by a band of mariachi players. Didn't that happen to you, too? No? Oh, what a pity. How sad for you!"

Having heard that story many times, all I can say is: lies, lies, all lies. It just doesn't happen that way, ladies. Yes, he can whisk you away. And yes, he can surprise you. But you don't just commit to marriage without discussing it first. To imply you never talked about getting engaged until it magically happened is ridiculous. When you're in a relationship and you want to make plans for the night, you discuss them. You check first with your guy. And you come to a conclusion together. That is what couples do. They communicate their desires, likes, and dislikes. Surprises can happen. And I hope they do. Who doesn't love surprises? But when it comes to your relationship, you have to feel comfortable enough to express what you

Jessica Kaminsky

need and want from your guy. Otherwise, you may have a long wait ahead of you.

As far as genuine surprises go, I can tell you that of all the women I interviewed for this book, there was only one (that's right, one) who had dated her boyfriend for only a month before he proposed. So that's one out of a hundred. Which is why this fantasy that proposals are made without the slightest bit of provocation only makes it harder for the women who are patiently waiting for their guy to come around on his own.

But the point of this chapter isn't simply to dispel the myth of the perfect proposal. It's to reassure you that you're *allowed* to bring up the subject of marriage. You're encouraged to mention your desire to get engaged. And you're even welcome to suggest that it happen sooner rather than later. These are all legitimate topics. They may not be received well (brace yourself), but discussing them is within your rights as an equal member of your relationship. Think about it: In every other aspect of your life (both personally and professionally) you do not shy away from expressing yourself and articulating your goals. So why not apply that same model to your relationship?

Some women still operate under the assumption that mentioning our interest in getting engaged is too pushy or aggressive. Not so, ladies. You just have to have a thick skin and be patient. When I told my husband (then boyfriend), Dave, that I wanted to get engaged and I wanted it to happen by the end of the year, he got defensive, accusing me of "taking the wind out of his sails."

"But there was no wind," I told him.

"Yeah, well . . . how would you know?" Dave said.

Only now that I'm on the other side do I see that Dave was not only scared by the prospect of change and how it would affect our relationship, but also frustrated at being told what to do.

So while many of us are uncomfortable with the idea of applying pressure on our significant others and becoming *that* girl (you know which girl I'm talking about), the flip side is that guys aren't always dodging the question. In some cases, they are planning to propose. They just take their time. And time can be the enemy. Take Helen, for example. She and her boyfriend, Billy, had been dating for three years when she decided that she was ready to get engaged. So she started to drop hints. First casually, then more

Jessica Kaminsky

overtly. Finally, Billy snapped. He didn't need to be told what to do. He had heard her the first time. Helen remembers being shocked. Since so many of her comments had fallen on deaf ears, how was she supposed to know that he had been listening all along?

But she had known Billy long enough to know that he had to do things his way. He was a traditionalist. He had heard her and he knew that this was something that was important to her. Now she had to give him the space, time, and freedom to actually get it done. So, just remember, when you're feeling frustrated at the snail's pace (or no pace) at which your guy is moving, try your very best to give him the benefit of the doubt.

How to Introduce the Subject of Marriage

A recently married friend told me about the approach she took with her then-boyfriend in introducing the subject of marriage. She calls it the Goldfish Theory. She believes that acclimating your boyfriend to marriage is not unlike making a goldfish comfortable in a new fish tank. When you bring the little fella home in a bag of water, you don't just drop him into the tank.

27

He could go into shock, right? So you keep him in the bag, letting him slowly get used to the temperature of the water, the other fish, the treasure chest, and the shipwrecked skeleton. In other words, you let him adjust to his new surroundings. You let him feel in control. Only then do you open up the bag and let the goldfish swim in the tank he now considers home.

If you handle your boyfriend as artfully as you do your fish, he will get comfortable with the idea of marriage instead of going into a state of panic. And if you're really skilled, he might even think he came up with the idea on his own.

Effective ways of hinting

There's nothing like the subtle art of suggestion when it comes to planting the seed in your boyfriend's head that the time has come to get engaged. At first, you may not feel comfortable dropping hints about your deep desire to sport something sparkly on your finger. Or you may not have full confidence in his ability to interpret your hints. (I refer you to the sparkly Michael Jackson glove he purchased for you on eBay that now resides in a box in your closet. Yes, it is indeed shiny, but not exactly what you had in mind.) Either way, time is passing by and you'd like to know if he shares your vision for a future together. But you're not the type of girlfriend to just tell him what you want. You would rather let him get there on his own. However, as you will soon learn, this may take a long time. You can try to wait it out. By all means, go ahead. . . . I'll just see you back here in chapter 2 when you're ready to take some action.

Subtle techniques

✳ Mention another friend who recently got engaged.

✳ Accidentally leave a magazine flipped open to a Harry Winston diamond ad.

✳ Loudly compliment a friend's ring within earshot of your guy.

✳ Take him to an antique store and casually wind your way to the jewelry counter.

✳ Emphasize that you *are* a diamond girl. (I mean, who isn't?)

✳ Tell him that you think huge diamonds are vulgar, if money is a concern. Really distasteful. So *not* you.

It's Time for . . . The Talk

It seems that the subtle approach didn't work and no matter how many hints you artfully drop, he still isn't getting it. So it's time to sit the numskull down for a little one-on-one. It's no one's favorite thing to do, but sometimes the direct approach is the only way to go. Now, there may not be one right way to bring up the *M* word, but here are a few suggestions for ways to avoid a fight.

Whatever you do, don't have The Talk on an empty stomach.

This discussion is never a short one, no matter what the outcome. So don't get serious on an empty stomach. It will only lead to unnecessary tears and tension. Low blood sugar has been known to be the leading cause of many a couple's fight. And usually they're just trying to figure out where to have brunch. So do yourself a favor—eat first, then talk.

Can't pin him down? Box him in.

Remember when you were little and your mother would get you in the car, where you couldn't flee, and then spring something on you? Well, she was no dummy and neither are you. If you're dating someone who is notoriously hard to pin down, and you want answers, then it's time to get creative about where and how you bring up ye olde desire to get engaged. Whether it's a road trip or a plane ride, you will have his attention . . . at least for the duration of the journey.

Don't be shy. Have a cocktail or two.
But not three.

I find that I'm always looser after a glass of wine. Less inhibited. Less anxious. And, dare I say, more articulate? Everything sounds better with a glass of wine in your hand. Think of it this way: You can either toast to your future together, or you can start checking out the guy at the end of the bar—if the discussion turned out to be disappointing, the single life may not be far behind. As far as I can tell, it's a win-win. Although a word to the wise, too many cocktails may make for some rather regrettable behavior. So loosen up but don't fall down drunk.

Keep your expectations low.

Not unlike the word "colonoscopy," the word "marriage" has been known to send a shiver of fear down most men's spines. They'll stutter and stammer and say anything to buy time. So, if you're expecting your guy to break into a huge grin and agree to all of your hopes and wishes, well . . . don't hold your breath. It takes time for men to warm up to the idea of spending the rest of their lives with one woman no matter how amazing she is or how much he loves her. So try looking at it this way: You have officially put the topic on the table and are one step closer to a resolution. Trust me, he'll come around. And if he doesn't, then it's better to find out sooner rather than later.

Make it short and sweet.

You're sharing your hopes and dreams, but you're also exposing yourself. Your defenses are down. So don't start backpedaling out of what you really want and don't ramble just to fill the deafening silence. Say your piece and slowly back away. Let your words sink in, leaving no room for the gray area to cloud your progress.

Jessica Kaminsky

Try not to break down in tears.

This is a tough one. Tears are the *X* factor. You never know when they're going to rear their ugly heads. But try your best to maintain control. You may well up out of relief or you may find yourself tearing up because he's saying all the wrong things. Whatever the reason, try to keep it together. The last thing you want is his pity when discussing your future together.

Ultimatums

Now, ultimatums aren't for everyone. And there are plenty of people who feel that an old-fashioned threat can take the romance right out of an impending proposal. But I'm of the belief that if you are fed up and damn tired of fighting all the time about everything except what you really want to talk about—getting engaged—then by all means, speak up. Your relationship demands it.

Need a new spin on the ultimatum concept? Think of it this way. You are issuing a challenge for your guy to propose. "I challenge you to a proposal, man who scratches himself in public and spends all Sunday in his boxers!" And who knows?

Maybe he'll surprise you and rise to the occasion. Stranger things have been known to happen.

Now for the balls out approach . . .

* Set a deadline and let him know the clock is ticking.

* Tear out the picture of the ring you want from a magazine and let him know that if it isn't on your finger by a certain date, then you walk.

* Suggest a day trip to the second floor of Tiffany's to browse their collection. There is a certain salesman you want your boyfriend to meet.

* Tired of waiting? Propose to him yourself. Hey, Pink did it.

Excuses, Excuses

You may have already talked about marriage, how many kids you want to have together, and that gorgeous house in the Hollywood Hills with the eat-in kitchen, hot tub, and views of the city that would make the perfect newlywed nest. But that was pillow

Jessica Kaminsky

talk. It meant nothing. It was the beginning of the relationship, and you were playing house. So don't be surprised if you hear some clichéd excuses when the subject of marriage is reintroduced.

When I first brought up the fact that I was ready to get engaged, Dave stared straight ahead and told me that he "didn't believe in marriage."

"What? Since when?"

"Always," he said.

"That is such a lie," I told him. I was livid. Furthermore, even if he didn't believe in marriage, shouldn't he have maybe mentioned that, oh . . . four years ago? And didn't he see how hard it was for me to put myself out there like that? The least he could have done was lie a little. But instead he tossed me the old "I don't believe in marriage" bone and I wanted to club him with it. Maybe a good boyfriend beating would make the pain and anger go away.

That was my emotional response. Anger, then concern for our future, followed by more anger. But my rational response, while confused and frustrated, was more forgiving. I asked questions like "Since when do you not believe in marriage?" And "Where does that feeling come from?" I patiently heard out his answers and then explained how I felt. Eventually we got to the heart of the matter. Dave had seen a lot of marriages fail. He didn't want ours to be one of those. So he figured if things remained the same, we couldn't fall into the same pitfalls. Very reasonable. I understood where he was coming from. But still, I wanted to get married, and slowly, over time, he came around to my way of thinking. It wasn't easy, but we got there and so will you.

Here are a few of the excuses you might hear along the way. . . .

"Marriage is just a slip of paper."

This is the excuse that Betsy heard when she first mentioned her desire to get married to Sam.

Emotional response: Initially she was frustrated, and then she was annoyed. Since when did Sam think marriage was just a slip of paper? Not only had they been dating for three years, but they'd recently been averaging a wedding a month, traveling all around the country to watch Sam's friends exchanging vows. So . . . shouldn't his views on marriage have come up a wee bit sooner? And if this was how he really felt, Betsy was pissed. She wanted to get married and Sam knew it. So if he was unwilling to budge on the issue, this might be a deal breaker.

Rational response: After the dust settled, Betsy took a step back and came to the conclusion that Sam's comment was simply a stalling tactic. To her, the discussion of marriage was inevitable, whereas Sam had felt blindsided by it. He was on a slower track than Betsy and his "marriage is just a slip of paper" excuse was just his knee-jerk reaction. And after they discussed the issue again, Betsy vowed to take a less aggressive, more sympathetic approach as long as Sam understood that she wanted to get married sometime before the next millennium.

"I thought you wanted to live together first."

This is the reason John gave Rachel as to why there was no engagement in the works.

John and Rachel had been dating for a long time—close to six years—and both were tired of shuttling their stuff back and forth from one place to the other. So they began to talk about the possibility of selling their respective places and buying something together.

But before they made such a move, Rachel sat John down and delicately explained that she wasn't going to be participating in any kind of real-estate venture without first getting engaged. She was firm on the subject and felt it was a very reasonable stipulation. But John clearly had a different idea of how the whole marriage thing would go down.

Emotional response: Rachel didn't even know she felt that way until the moment they first started discussing the prospect of living together. She had never considered herself a traditional person. In fact, just the opposite. And so she had surprised even herself when she told John that she wouldn't move in with him unless they were engaged. It was unlike her to be so direct on the subject of marriage. But this is what she wanted. And she also knew that if they did move in together before they got engaged, it might be another six years before they talked about marriage. And she definitely did not want that. As for John's response, she was not surprised. Marriage was something they had barely discussed. But she was ready and he needed to know that.

Rational response: After their discussion, Rachel realized that they probably wouldn't be getting engaged anytime soon. But she was happy to have at least floated the subject by John. That way, the next time she brought it up he wouldn't look like a deer caught in headlights. And . . . maybe John would surprise her. Hey, it could happen.

"I need to be further along in my career before I even consider marriage."

This is the excuse Jenny heard when she first mentioned her interest in getting engaged to her boyfriend, Peter.

Emotional response: A close friend of theirs had just gotten engaged and the subject of marriage was in the air. Jenny brought it up, and that's when Peter dropped his priceless gem about needing to be further along in his career. He was already doing well as far as she was concerned. He had just been given a promotion. How much farther up the ladder did he need to be? At the time, it seemed so abstract. And Jenny felt floored by Peter's lack of enthusiasm.

Rational response: Jenny sat down with Peter and expressed her concern regarding his marital hesitation. He told her that his desire to wait had stemmed from a need to be more financially solvent. He then explained that when he was a kid, his parents had lost their money in a series of bad investments and he vowed never to repeat their mistake. Afterward Jenny saw where Peter was coming from and was much more understanding of his need to wait.

Saving Face

Have you ever had one of those moments when you were expecting a candlelit dinner, a romantic walk in the park, or a hillside picnic resulting in an amazing engagement story to share with all of your closest friends, and instead to your shock and embarrassment it all unfolded very, very differently? These women share their miscalculated moments and how they did their best to save face in the wake of no proposal.

Jane

It was Jane's birthday and her boyfriend Matthew was taking her out for dinner. The restaurant had an over-the-top theatrical element—overly attentive waiters, lovey-dovey couples at every table, impeccable service. Jane could just tell—an engagement was imminent.

When they sat down, Matthew ordered a fabulous bottle of wine. Clearly, he was sparing no expense and all Jane could think was: Is he going to ask me now? Or is he going to ask me later? She could hardly wait.

Jane barely remembers what they talked about during dinner. She was just waiting to get to dessert. She was certain Matthew would be proposing then. Finally the meal came to an end and a gaggle of waiters approached carrying a cake with a sparkler in it. It was a magical moment. As the cake was placed in front of Jane, she closed her eyes and made a wish. She wished that she would love the ring Matthew had picked out for her. And as if on cue, Matthew reached into his pocket, and pulled out a velvet box. Jane melted. "Oh, Matthew." The waiters gasped.

Jane looked around. She wanted to savor everything about this moment. What song was playing in the background, the look on Matthew's face, the overjoyed woman in the corner. Matthew then opened the box, turning it toward her. "I hope you like . . . diamond earrings," Matthew said. Diamond earrings?! Diamond fucking earrings?! That was his big surprise? Jane could feel her eyes welling up with tears. What kind of idiot would ever give a woman earrings in a box so obviously suited for an engagement ring? She couldn't believe it.

Matthew could tell something was not right. But she refused to break down. Instead a flood of adrenaline kicked in. She had to save face. "What's wrong?" Matthew asked. Jane looked at the earrings. "I guess I'm just not really a diamond girl. Too flashy." Lies, lies, lies. Couldn't he see she was lying through her teeth? But Matthew couldn't. And Jane kept the charade alive to save face. A week later the diamond earrings were returned and a watch was bought in its place.

Kelly

Kelly and John were getting ready to take their first vacation together. And while Kelly knew where they were going (Hawaii), John had been the one to plan all the details of the trip. He was being very secretive about the whole thing. But occasionally she'd overhear him on the phone, booking the "Sea Ranch Cottage" with the "ocean views." Kelly wasn't the type to jump to conclusions. But since their anniversary would be happening during their trip, there was a teeny, tiny part of her that thought they might get engaged. But ever practical, Kelly pushed those thoughts out of her head.

And so, Kelly and John set off for Hawaii. The hotel was beautiful, their room was spectacular, and at night they'd go to sleep to the sound of the waves hitting the beach. Everything was perfect. Finally their anniversary rolled around and they went out to dinner. John was staring at her all affectionately. Their bottle of wine had just arrived and John held up his glass of wine. He told her that he had something important to say. *Oh my God*, Kelly thought. *This is it.* He told her how amazing he thought she was, and how these past three years had been the best years of his life. She was literally on the edge of her seat. She just wanted to make sure she looked surprised when he pulled the ring out of his pocket. John turned to her and said, "I hope we have three more perfect years just like this." They clinked glasses. And that was it. No ring. No present, even. Just a toast.

Kelly's eyes started to well up with tears. When he asked her if everything was all right, she just said that she loved him so much and was moved by the moment.

That night, unable to hold it in, she had a total melt-down in the hotel room. Screaming, crying, a full-blown tantrum, which she played off the next day as depression at their impending departure. John bought the lie. And a few months later, after many a discussion of where the relationship was heading, they broke up. Kelly doesn't regret a thing.

Straight from the Horse's Mouth

My married friend Josh offers up a male perspective on what he went through on the bumpy road to "I do."

Did your lady give you an ultimatum (propose by this date or else)? And if so, how did it make you feel?

There were a lot of ultimatums handed out during that pre-engagement time. But I didn't take them that seriously. Not that she didn't mean what she said. It was more like I didn't think that I'd come home one day and she'd be gone. But when it came to getting engaged, she wanted it to happen now. Not down the road, not in a month. Right now. It could have upset me, but I decided to make a

44

choice. I could get angry and be part of the problem. Or
I could assure her that I loved her and it would happen
eventually. But it wasn't going to be overnight.

SOME ENGAGING HISTORY

———

* The word "diamond" originates from
the Greek word "adamant," which means
steadfast or invincible. This is how diamonds,
which were known to be indestructible, got
their name.

* The average cost of an engagement ring
is $3,165.00.

* One in five men propose on bended knee.

He Said/She Said

Real-life couples share what brought them together and made their relationships work.

Derek & Tammy

They met in 1999 and dated for five years before getting engaged. This is their story.

ACT ONE

Classroom Courtship

He said: Derek first spotted Tammy in a business class he was taking. But he didn't pay much attention to her. Derek was a second-year student, taking a first-year class, which he had signed up for because of the teacher. So he wasn't there to bond with his fellow students.

It wasn't until a party a few weeks later that he and Tammy first talked. He thought she was cute and had an easygoing way about her. They were making small talk when Derek, thinking he was being subtle, asked what year she had graduated from college. "Oh, so you want to know how old I am?" Tammy asked. Derek tried to cover, but she was right, that was exactly what he was trying to do. He liked that she saw right through him.

She said: Things were a little more complicated for Tammy when she first met Derek. For one, she was still living with her boyfriend. It had begun as one of those "save money on the rent" propositions. But of course, she wasn't a roommate, helping out with the rent. She was a girlfriend who had grown increasingly dissatisfied with her current relationship. And then there was the small matter of their shared dog, Rufus.

Sometime in the middle of the semester Tammy ended things with her then-boyfriend and moved out. Around that time, she and Derek started spending more time together. At first they were just friends. She enjoyed his company and he made her laugh. But it wasn't until Tammy took a trip out of town that her feelings for Derek really started to take shape. She had brought her bags to class and she remembers walking to the back of the classroom to say good-bye to Derek. She intended just to give him a hug. But instead she bent down and kissed him. As she left the classroom, she thought to herself, "I just kissed Derek. Why did I just kiss Derek?" It was as if her body was one step ahead of her mind.

While she was away, Tammy remembers thinking a lot about Derek. Here she was on a tropical vacation with three single friends and all she could do was wonder what Derek was up to. And when she got off the plane she called him on the way home from the airport. They agreed to meet that night. Derek had given up smoking and drinking for Lent. So their first date consisted of seltzers at a diner a few blocks from her house. From that point on, they started seeing each other. They didn't want to rush into anything. After all, Tammy was newly single. But mainly, they didn't want to ruin the friendship.

Not long after, Tammy introduced Derek to her mother and sister, who were in town visiting. It was a high-pressure situation, and he handled it beautifully. He brought pink tulips for her mother, which Tammy loved. Derek was thoughtful and classy without being calculated or contrived.

ACT TWO
Slow and Steady

Derek and Tammy were together for about two years before the subject of marriage first came up. It was around that time, Tammy noticed, that people began to feel comfortable commenting on the status of their relationship. When were they going to get engaged?

And what were their plans for the future? On the one hand, the marriage question seemed practical. But on the other hand, why was it anyone else's business?

She said: Tammy did her best to brush off people's questions. She wasn't ready to get married and yet the constant barrage of questions had invaded her psyche and she found herself wondering: How did Derek feel? Had he ever thought about marriage? And if so, was it with her? But before she let herself get too worked up, she'd remember that marriage hadn't even been on her radar until someone else brought it up. Besides, she knew that they weren't ready. Well, Derek wasn't ready.

Derek was still living the life of a teenager. He'd stay out late with his friends, and then he'd sleep until noon. She just couldn't imagine that he was even close to taking that next step. And she was all right with that. Well . . . in theory. Truthfully, it wasn't until she realized how long it might take to further their relationship that she found herself feeling frustrated. What *was* their plan for the future? But she refused to be the one to bring it up. Besides, in so many ways, she was totally content. They had fun together. They made each other laugh. And they were very loving. Derek just had other priorities. And she couldn't change that. So she had to be patient (for now) and wait.

He said: Derek knew within the first year that he wanted to marry Tammy. But Tammy wasn't one to jump into things without careful consideration. So Derek chose to follow her lead and take things slowly. Time passed and they were enjoying being together. Derek even asked if Tammy wanted to move in with him.

She said: Tammy remembers how she phrased her response to Derek's request for her to move in with him. She told him that she didn't want to move in unless she was married. She wasn't saying that she needed to be married to him tomorrow. She wanted to marry Derek, she just didn't want to apply that kind of pressure.

ACT THREE
Internal Dialogue, Eternal Struggle

Another year passed by and Derek and Tammy were still dating. Things were status quo. And that's when an apartment in Derek's building became available. He immediately thought of Tammy and told her that

Jessica Kaminsky

she should check it out even though she had a place of her own. But why, Tammy wanted to know. Then Derek explained that if she lived above him, they could each have their own space but still be close to each other. And that's when Tammy lost it.

She said: Even before Derek brought up the apartment, she'd been having this internal dialogue, vacillating between hope and despair. Hope that she and Derek would get engaged and that everything would fall into place. And despair that maybe she was wrong and nothing would ever change. Perhaps Derek was this eternal bachelor, meant to roam the earth forever alone. So when he suggested that she move into the shabby apartment above him, he confirmed all of her worst fears. He wasn't interested in moving forward. He wanted a neighbor, not a wife. Tammy envisioned that if she took the apartment, they would enter into this hippie existence, have tons of children who'd wander the halls wearing ill-fitting diapers and smearing peanut butter on the walls, and they'd never get married.

And if that wasn't enough, when she told Derek that she wasn't going to move into the apartment upstairs, he said that he was going to offer it to his best friend. *Great*, Tammy thought, *now that he's starting a frat house, we're really never going to get married. Ever!* She excused herself and went to take a walk to blow off steam. She fumed. She sulked. She cried. Nothing helped.

He said: After Derek brought up the vacant apartment in his building, he immediately sensed that something was wrong. He could see it in her eyes. He asked Tammy if she wanted to talk about it. But she said no. Finally, Tammy agreed to discuss what was upsetting her. After a few deep breaths, Tammy opened up. She needed to know where they were in their relationship. They had been together for three years, going on four. What was happening? Derek wasn't surprised by her question. He had been expecting this for some time and told her that he wanted to further the relationship but that he needed to straighten his life out first.

LOOKING BACK

It was a difficult conversation for both of them, but it helped clear up a lot of unanswered questions. And

Tammy felt relieved. She still couldn't understand why Derek's life had to be in perfect order before he could consider marriage. It was as if he didn't think he deserved a wife or a life until he had a suitable job. But the fact that they had finally broached the subject filled her with hope. And she decided to give him a year.

ACT FOUR
How Tammy Learned to Drive

Six Months Later: Summer was approaching and Derek and Tammy were planning a trip to visit his family in the Berkshires. They were both looking forward to getting out of the sweaty city.

She said: After many months of successfully putting the whole engagement issue out of her head, Tammy could feel her frustration beginning to creep back in. So she made a pact with herself. If nothing happened by the end of the summer, she'd bring up the subject again. But she wasn't going to be happy about it.

Then something vaguely hopeful occurred as they were standing on the subway platform. Derek mentioned a friend of his who had just proposed to his girlfriend. Apparently his friend had been getting a lot of pressure from his disgruntled lady. Derek was grumbling about how it just wasn't right. Tammy shrugged. Sometimes people need to be reminded, she said. Derek turned to her, "Well, I don't need to be reminded." Now, some people might have taken that as hostile or snippy. But Tammy knew Derek well enough to understand what he was saying: Don't say anything because I have something in the works. Or at least that's what she hoped.

He said: It was Memorial Day weekend and Tammy and Derek set off for the Berkshires. One of the underlining goals of the trip was to teach Tammy, a lifelong New Yorker, how to drive. She was pretty grumpy about it. What she didn't know was that Derek was in possession of an engagement ring, a single-carat solitaire-setting diamond from Tiffany. As he patted his jacket pocket for the hundredth time, he began to feel himself getting increasingly nervous. He hadn't even thought about what he was going to say.

She said: When they arrived at Derek's parents' place, his mom put them in a room with separate beds. She felt like a ten-year-old having a sleepover and that nothing was ever going to change. Tammy was in a

Jessica Kaminsky

bad mood. Then there was that damn driving lesson Derek kept insisting she take. Why did she have to learn to drive so badly? Couldn't she just continue taking the subway?

THE VERDICT

Derek surprised Tammy with a ring after a particularly difficult driving lesson. She had caused a traffic jam and nearly hit another car, so a marriage proposal was the last thing she was expecting. She just thought Derek wanted her to pull over because he didn't want her behind the wheel anymore. Well . . . that was part of the reason. But the other part was that they were next to a beautiful, picturesque lake. Once they made it out to the dock, Derek dropped to one knee and proposed. She said yes, but she couldn't stop laughing. She was so happy. Then they shared a bottle of champagne that Derek's mom had tossed in the trunk of the car. They drank warm bubbly and giggled about their future together. They were married six months later.

EVERY GUY NEEDS "A GUY"

Once Derek decided that he was ready to propose, the next step was getting a ring. But he didn't even know where to begin. In the back of his mind, he remembered someone saying something about the "diamond district." But the details were vague, and when he got there, he felt totally overwhelmed. There were too many people shouting at him, trying to lure them into their boutiques. And Derek wasn't versed enough in diamonds to know if he was getting a deal or if he was getting ripped off.

The one thing he did know was that he needed "a guy." He needed someone to walk him through the process. Someone to help him out, educate him, and give him the attention and respect that such a huge purchase deserved. For God's sake, this was the most money he had ever spent! He had bought a car for less. This wasn't a casual purchase. For Derek, this ring represented everything—his love for Tammy, his belief in their future, and his ability to buy her something worthy of being on her finger every day. At last Derek found his "guy," in the form of a salesman at Tiffany. His name was Duncan. Duncan was honest and relaxed. Warm, but not slick. Duncan guided him through the process. And in the end, Derek felt confident about his purchase and swears up and down that every guy needs "a guy."

Rock Talk: Let's Break It Down

✳ There is no foolproof way to broach the rock. Relationships don't come with guarantees.

✳ When in doubt, go with the Goldfish Theory.

✳ Let him know that you want an answer. Don't beat around the bush. Be direct. Come out and ask him: "Hey, buddy, do you get that I want to get married or what?"

✳ Not happy with his inability to commit? Don't be afraid to go balls out and throw down an ultimatum.

✳ Brace yourself for a barrage of insulting excuses.

✳ Repeat after me: Do not take it personally. Do not take it personally.

✳ Remember, "I don't believe in marriage" doesn't always mean "I don't believe in marriage." Sometimes it just means "I'm freaking out. And I'm trying to buy some time."

DON'T ROCK THE BOAT

If It Ain't Broke, Don't Fix It

This chapter is devoted to those couples who are rock-steady but don't feel that nagging need to formalize their love with a ring or a wedding. You never have to worry about whether or not they'll break up—they're in it for the long haul. Marriage is just not their cup of tea. And it's not because they're avoiding making a lifetime commitment to each other. Hardly. They are just so secure in their relationship, they don't need to be married. They're on a whole other level.

And frankly, I'm a little jealous. Not that I didn't have that kind of faith and confidence in my relationship.

I did. But I still wanted the bells and whistles. I needed the ring on my finger and the over-the-top yet tasteful wedding my parents could brag about. I wish I were cool enough to forgo all of those traditional trappings. But alas, this is who I am. Not these rock-steady folk, though. They're buying houses, having babies, and making future plans together all without the marriage label. And they find it works just fine for them. But whatever you do, don't call them husband and wife.

Rockabye Baby

Some couples would sooner have a child together than ever get married. Here is a story of one such couple.

Natalie & Charlie

For years Natalie didn't like going to weddings. She'd cringe every time she heard about another one of her friends gearing up to walk down the aisle. It wasn't that she wasn't happy for her friends; she was. It was more that she was mad at herself. Mad at the long hours she worked and angry at the job she blamed for keeping her from meeting someone.

But after years of weddings Natalie had a break-through. She stopped caring if she was next and settled into the idea that she might never meet her mate. Not that she was giving up. It was more that she wasn't going to sit on the sidelines anymore and wait for her life to start. In fact, she had just bought a house—something she had been hesitant to do for years because she felt strange making such a big purchase alone. But Natalie was practical and it made sense.

Also she had started talking with a gay friend of hers about the idea of having a child together. More than anything, Natalie wanted to be a mother. She was getting up there in age and didn't want to miss her window of opportunity to have a kid just because she wasn't in a relationship with someone.

ACT ONE

Excuse Me, Is Anyone Sitting There?

She said: One day Natalie was working with her TV writing partner at a coffee shop when a guy sat down next to her. They all started talking, and he introduced himself. His name was Charlie and he was an actor. Ugh. Eye roll. Groan. Natalie couldn't have been less interested. But he was sweet and interesting, and he had the dreamiest smile. And then when he quoted from an episode of *Alias* that she and her partner had written, that was it—Natalie was a goner. Next thing she knew she was happily sharing a scone and a chocolate-chip cookie with a complete stranger.

He said: When asked what he remembered about meeting Natalie, Charlie answers immediately. Her eyes. Her beautiful blue eyes. That, and she kicked his ass in a game of pickup basketball back at her place. From that moment on, Charlie was hooked. She was totally different from the women he had dated in the past. She was relaxed, funny, comfortable in her own skin. She was like a breath of fresh air.

ACT TWO
Lost Weekends and Lost Sleep

After their initial encounter, Natalie and Charlie started dating casually. He had been burned by a bad divorce and wasn't looking to settle down.

She said: Normally, Charlie's desire to keep things loose would have set off all kinds of alarms for Natalie. A man with emotional scars, commitment issues, and a slew of animals (a bird, three cats, and a dog, to be

THE TRUTH BEHIND THE ROCK

exact), all inherited from the divorce. But due to her recent decision to try and have a baby with her friend, she felt oddly liberated and was experiencing a new sense of calm and purposefulness. Why couldn't she have a casual, fun, flirty fling like a character from *Sex and the City*? So she told Charlie that he was free to date other people. In fact, she would too.

But neither of them seemed interested in anyone else and soon they started spending more and more time together. And whenever Natalie would start to panic (Where is this going? How does he feel about me? Am I going to get hurt?), she would reassure herself: Charlie wasn't seeing anyone else. In fact, he wasn't even trying. So instead of listening to what he was saying, Natalie decided to focus on Charlie's actions.

He said: For Charlie, it was a camping trip that he and Natalie took very early in their relationship that forever changed the way he felt about her. He had initially suggested going on the trip as a way to distract Natalie, who was waiting to hear about a new job and was feeling anxious. But right from the beginning, things did not go according to plan. Halfway to the mountains, her car broke down and it started to rain. But to Charlie's surprise, Natalie didn't get upset or freaked out. She took everything in stride, from the crappy motel in the middle of nowhere to the fact that her car wouldn't be ready for three days. And because Natalie kept her sense of humor and didn't let things upset her, what could have been a disaster ended up being a fantastic trip. They played Scrabble, watched old movies, and ate diner food. And then, when her car was eventually fixed, they scrapped their initial plans in favor of heading north for a baseball game. Charlie loved Natalie's easygoing attitude and her spontaneity. In his opinion, this trip took them to a whole other level.

ACT THREE

The Talk

It was about six months into dating that Natalie found herself sitting down with Charlie for the dreaded relationship "talk." What were they doing? Did they have a future together or was it time to cut their losses and pull up anchor? After many late-night discussions, she and Charlie decided to see each other exclusively. Love was in the air. But the bigger question still loomed—if she was getting this serious about Charlie, was she still going to try and have a baby with her friend?

It didn't take long for Natalie to decide that she would not be having a baby with her friend. But what took everyone by surprise was when she and Charlie decided that *they* would try to get pregnant. Yes, they were technically rushing it. But as far as they were concerned, they had bigger fish to fry. They both wanted kids. And since they were both approaching forty, they had to act swiftly. And no matter what, Natalie and Charlie felt confident that however things ended (if ever) between them, they could be certain that they would be amazing parents and they would always be there for their child.

ACT FOUR
Baby Time

Natalie expected that it would take some time to conceive. She had never been pregnant before, not even a false alarm. Secretly, she was convinced she and Charlie would be flying to China to adopt a baby by the end of the year. But they got pregnant on the first try.

Jessica Kaminsky

Baby mama: Even though they had decided not to get married, Natalie still wanted a ring or some kind of token from Charlie. She was working with all these women who were sporting these enormous rocks that could double as hand weights while she had nothing. And she refused to look like the unloved pregnant woman. Besides, she didn't want to be hit on anymore. (Yes, Natalie actually got hit on throughout her pregnancy.) So Charlie decided to design her a ring. It was made up of three bands braided together with a sapphire (Natalie's birthstone) in the middle. They called it the Eleanor Ring, after their daughter.

THE VERDICT

Natalie and Charlie are very much together. Like all couples, they have their moments, their issues, their frustrations. But they're committed to each other and to raising their beautiful daughter. And although they are not married, they consider themselves a family.

SOME ENGAGING HISTORY

✳ The word "betrothed" comes from the Anglo-Saxon word "troweth," meaning truth. Betrothed means to "give a truth or pledge" and thus, an engagement ring became the outward indication that a woman had pledged her love to one man.

✳ In A.D. 860, Pope Nicholas I decreed that an engagement ring was a requirement of marital intent. And the engagement ring had to be made of gold, which would signify a financial sacrifice on the part of the prospective husband.

✳ The ancient Greeks believed that diamonds were bits or splinters of stars that had fallen to earth.

Jessica Kaminsky

He Said/She Said

Real-life couples share what brought them together and made their relationships work.

Amelia & Diego

Amelia and Diego met in high school but didn't start dating until after college. This is their story.

ACT ONE

How To Make Something Familiar Feel Fresh

One of the biggest hurdles for Amelia and Diego was simply that they had known each other since freshman year of high school. They had been study buddies and lab partners. They had passed notes in Ms. Shea's history class and had shared bagels in the food zone. They were friends in high school, then best friends in college, but they had always dated other people. It wasn't until they graduated that something shifted in their dynamic. They went from being friends to being one of the nerdy couples they used to make fun of.

Of course, in the beginning there was that typical new relationship awkwardness. They knew each other incredibly well, and yet once they started dating it was as if they knew nothing about one another. Plus, Amelia couldn't help but feel vaguely embarrassed that she was dating someone she had gone to high school with. It felt so . . . well, high school. But they got over it. And here they are eight years later.

ACT TWO
Another One Bites the Dust

Along the way, Amelia and Diego have watched as many of their close friends first got engaged, then married. Last year, they went to five weddings. The year before that, they went to four. And for a couple that apparently had little interest in marriage, I couldn't help but wonder what effect all of these weddings were having on them. Was the experience positive? Negative? A mere blip on their radar that barely registered at all? Or did the engagements, then weddings, just reaffirm their distaste for the whole idea of marriage?

He said: Diego doesn't have any particular disdain for marriage—he could take it or leave it. He has more of an "it's none of my business" perspective when it comes to other people's decisions to marry. Diego believes that marriage is between two people and that each couple's commitment to the relationship manifests itself in its own way—far be it from him to judge whether it's right for them or not. For him, marriage is a bit like law school—it's the next obvious step if you don't know what else to do with your life.

She said: Amelia, on the other hand, began to view the various engagements, then the subsequent weddings, in a different sort of light. Yes, it was true that attending numerous weddings would inevitably cause the issue of marriage to bubble to the surface. But Amelia liked their relationship the way it was and had begun to enjoy feeling different. Besides, there were few marriages that she could call genuine successes. In her opinion, a good marriage involved a level of suppleness, while the bad marriages tended to be more rigid. In general, her problem with marriage, and why she's not interested in it, is that she already feels like a conventional, law-abiding, Goody Two-shoes (with a college degree, career, house, and dog) and she doesn't need another societal convention to tighten her world. For now, the idea of *not* getting

THE TRUTH BEHIND THE ROCK

married feels like a way to maintain some crumb of resistance. But mostly, ever since Amelia decided to commit to her relationship for the long haul, marriage almost seems gratuitous.

He said: While Diego can see himself married one day—in fact, he already feels married—the concept of a successful marriage is hard for him to pin down. It seems to him that no long-term marriage can be labeled either a success or a failure. Newer marriages haven't yet withstood the test of time (which seems to be the real hurdle) and longer-standing ones are a total mixed bag. His parents have been married for thirty-five years and seem to be happier together now than they've ever been. They made sacrifices and probably gave up parts of themselves along the way while growing into a happy couple, but it was worth it to them.

ACT THREE
The New Contract

An interesting thing happened to Amelia and Diego. As their friends started to get engaged, they realized that while marriage may not be in the immediate

Jessica Kaminsky

future for them, they needed to examine the state of their relationship. Thus, the new contract was born.

He said: The new contract came straight from the lips of Diego's therapist. She heard his story and said simply, "Oh, obviously, your contract is up. The terms you've been living under have expired. They're no longer relevant now. It's time for a new contract." This led to a long, uncomfortable conversation in a diner with Amelia. Over grilled cheese sandwiches, they candidly discussed their relationship, sharing their likes, dislikes, and concerns. Some things weren't easy to hear, while some were surprisingly reaffirming.

She said: According to Amelia, the new contract arose because they were having a lot of problems around the five-year mark. Amelia felt like she hadn't wholeheartedly committed to the relationship, and she was skeptical of Diego as well. So one night, after having another argument, they decided that they needed something substantive to show that they were really *in* this thing. So they came up with the idea of a contract, and then they elaborated on it. Amelia remembers the contract negotiations going like this:

"Well, there has to be some sort of ceremony, and I know my mom will want to come." "Well, then my parents are coming too." "Okay, then they should help pay for it." "If they are paying, then we should have a party." "Yeah, with dancing and lots of food." And on and on it went until they realized that they were in essence planning a wedding . . . only they had approached it from the back door.

Ultimately, they did not end up having their version of a wedding to celebrate the new contract. Instead, they went out to a nice dinner and toasted each other over a glass of wine.

THE VERDICT

Amelia and Diego concede that they may get married one day. They both think it would be cool for the kid that they plan to have someday to be at their wedding. But for now, they're content to share a house, a car, and a dog named Nero.

Rock Talk: Let's Break It Down

* Just because everyone is getting married doesn't mean that you have to.

* You can be rock-steady without a rock.

* Who cares what other people think if you aren't married and have a kid. If it's working for you, screw 'em.

* Honesty is the best policy with yourself and your partner.

* There isn't a specific life order. It doesn't always have to be marriage, house, kid. It can go house, kid, marriage—or even just kid.

* Oh, right. You're the adult. You make the rules.

STUCK BETWEEN A ROCK
AND A HARD PLACE

WE'VE ALL HAD THOSE RELATIONSHIPS ABOUT which, despite the glaring signs (your friends hate him, he's a jealous control freak, you fight constantly—both loudly and in public), you decide to dig in your heels and say, "I don't care what everyone else thinks. I am going to make this one work." And so you spend weeks, months, years pouring your energy into an unhealthy relationship, determined against all odds to fix it. Of course, it's no surprise to anyone when you eventually break up. But at the time, you were certain he was the guy for you. Too bad you didn't end it sooner, or at least before cheating on him with your next-door neighbor. But it takes a mature person to recognize those signs.

And so, many of us are doomed to go through the screaming, the yelling, and the name-calling until we either get wise and end it, or somehow push through to a satisfying new beginning.

The tough part is determining when that troubled relationship is worth fighting for and when it's time to walk away. Here, three women share their experiences with men they thought could be Mr. Right. Oh, how wrong they were.

Charlotte

Charlotte met Denny at the dog park. Her poodle and his bulldog were friends, so they would talk while their dogs sniffed each other. Eventually, Denny asked for Charlotte's number. They went on a date that Friday and got to know each other over giant bowls of pasta. Later that night, they made out like teenagers on the front steps of her house. Charlotte felt like this could be the start of something. When she told her friends about him, they cautioned her not to fall so quickly. But she dismissed their concerns. Besides, she was in total control. He adored her. She could tell.

So she and Denny started going on more dates. This led to sleepovers and several weekends away.

They would always have a great time together, but something seemed off and Charlotte couldn't understand why their relationship didn't seem to be gaining any momentum. They'd only see each other on Tuesday, Friday, and every other Sunday. Like clockwork. And if Charlotte ever suggested that they make plans on another night, Denny would always have a reason why he couldn't make it.

Charlotte tried not to be paranoid. She didn't want to come off as controlling or jealous, so she tried to relax and play it cool. And then, one night her girlfriend called. She had seen Denny kissing another girl at a bar. Charlotte was crushed. How could he do that to her?

When she confronted him, he told her that they weren't exclusive. He thought she knew that. She was free to date other men, just as he was free to date other women. And if she had a problem with that, then they should probably end it.

Now, the smart thing for Charlotte to do would have been to break up. But she liked Denny more than she was comfortable admitting. And while she wasn't crazy about the idea of sharing him, she was confident that she could win him over. So they continued to see each other on Tuesdays, Fridays, and every other Sunday.

On each date, she'd try her best to be winning, charming, and casually perfect. She wanted Denny to say, "I know I've been seeing other women. But it stops now!" But he never did say those things. And the truth was Charlotte wasn't comfortable sharing him. So she gave him his Tuesdays, Fridays, and every other Sunday back. And now she and her poodle go to a different dog park. It's a little farther away, but that's okay with them. They like it better that way.

Sarah

Sarah had been seeing Todd for the past six years—since her junior year of college. They had been through a lot together, and Todd was a great guy. Their relationship was comfortable, loving, and supportive. And she had always just assumed that she would spend the rest of her life with him. But recently, she'd been feeling like maybe there was more out there for her.

It had started with some casual, flirty banter with a coworker. And then she reconnected with an old boyfriend one night at a party. She hadn't done anything wrong . . . yet. But her mind was beginning to wander. She didn't want to hurt Todd's feelings. She loved him dearly, but she felt like she was twenty-six years old going on forty in this relationship and she didn't want to limit her experiences just because she was too chicken to tell her boyfriend the truth.

She felt too guilty to be honest and she was too nonconfrontational to end it. She tried pulling away, coming up with lame excuses why she couldn't see him. But he just assumed she was busy with work and didn't suspect a thing. And then she did the one thing she promised herself she would never do. She hurt him, badly. She cheated on him with some guy.

In her mind she needed to do something so awful that she wouldn't be able to look herself in the mirror, thus forcing her own hand. The next day, she told Todd what she had done. He was devastated and she felt like a coward. But she got what she wanted. At last, she was free.

Frances

Frances met Jacob at a cocktail party. She loved his nerdy, preppy style and quiet but strong presence. She didn't usually go for shy guys, but she loved the way he showered her with gifts and always made her feel like a princess. He was older than she was, which she had never considered to be an issue until he started insisting they leave parties early. He'd suddenly claim to not feel well and demand that they go home. Her friends would comment that Jacob didn't seem to like them. But she'd defend him, saying it took time to get to know him and that once they did, they would see just how charming and funny he could be. And she wasn't lying. Jacob was all of those things, but only for her. With everyone else in her life, he was reserved, even chilly, as if he had decided that these people weren't important enough for him to make the effort. Frances would try to get him to open up, but he remained distant. She couldn't under-stand how one person could be so warm to her and then so cold to the people she loved. Didn't he know the way to a girl's heart was through her girlfriends?

Jacob seemed like the perfect match for her in so many ways. Smart, successful, loving . . . but Frances was feeling increasingly isolated from her life. If he was everything she wanted, then why did she feel so lonely? She had to make a choice. She knew what she had to do—it was time for him to go.

THE TRUTH BEHIND THE ROCK

Here are a few signs that maybe, just maybe, he's not the right one for you:

✳ You find yourself thinking about someone else when you're kissing him (and we're not talking about Viggo—he's allowed). Instead it's your coworker with whom, unbeknownst to your boyfriend, you've been exchanging flirty, dirty e-mails for the past two months.

✳ You consistently have more fun with your other friends than with your boyfriend.

✳ Everything he does, from how he eats to the way he breathes, drives you *crazy*.

✳ You fight constantly.

✳ You read his journal, hoping to discover that he's cheating on you. He isn't. But he thinks you are. This gives you an idea. A bad one.

✳ You've resorted to faking orgasms just so that you can get back to watching the rest of an old *Seinfeld* episode.

✳ If you had to admit it, you'd have to say you're just not in love anymore.

Jessica Kaminsky

Straight from the Horse's Mouth

Wouldn't it be helpful if we could just climb into our guys' heads and understand what the hell they mean when they say, "It's not you. It's me"? Justin attempts to illuminate the situation for us.

You've had a few very serious relationships in your life. And you've lived with several women. Did you ever consider getting married to any of them? And if not, what are you waiting for?

It isn't that specific—like if only she had long hair and green eyes. Or, if only she were a Jewish intellectual from New York—then I would have found my soul mate. It's more intangible. I guess I'm kind of a relationship junkie. I feel like I'm at my best when I'm with someone else. I make more sense as a person. My nerdy quirks seem endearing, not annoying. As for marriage . . . I need to be involved with someone for a while before I feel like I really know who they are. And, of course, when you achieve that level of intimacy, you see all of her flaws. And she sees mine too. It's hard to explain. I guess if I was trying to pinpoint exactly what it was that I was looking for in a woman, I'd say she needed to be evolved. And that takes a certain degree of maturity. Anyone can be a princess, but to be a queen is sublime.

SOME ENGAGING HISTORY

✳ A pearl engagement ring is said to be bad luck because its shape mimics that of a tear.

✳ The right of any woman to propose on February 29 (on a leap year) goes back hundreds of years to when leap years were not recognized in English law. It was considered a day that had no legal status, and so it was a day to which tradition no longer applied. Therefore, women were free to propose to the man they wished to marry.

✳ You can have the remains of a loved one (a departed husband or loyal pet) turned into a diamond. It's creepy, but true. This is made possible because during cremation carbon is released, which can then be heated into graphite. The end result is a fancy-colored diamond composed of a loved one's remains. Hey, it's easier to carry around than an urn full of ashes.

✳ Diamonds were once believed to be deadly if swallowed.

Jessica Kaminsky

He Said/She Said

Introducing the now defunct . . .

Victoria & Jeremy

Victoria dated Jeremy for three years. They toyed with the idea of marriage and a life beyond scheduled sleepovers, but ultimately decided to end it. This is their story.

ACT ONE

Strangers in the Night

Victoria had been single for what felt like a very long time. She had been living in a small, economically depressed town, working for the local newspaper. While the job was challenging and at times rewarding, her life outside of work was nonexistent. Her immediate dating prospects consisted of the toothless man who drank beer out of a brown bag on her stoop and the pervy shopkeeper at the local deli. The nightlife was grim. So when a friend invited her to a party in the city, she jumped at the offer.

Victoria arrived at the party in a terrible mood. She had gotten into yet another fight with her mother, who was riding her about the way she dressed, which was "too messy," according to her mom, who considered this to be the major reason Victoria was having trouble finding a man. That and her refusal to get a weekly blowout at her mom's salon. Victoria sighed. Like it was that simple. But she was determined not to let her mom's comments ruin her night. She was going to have fun, no matter what.

Victoria was standing at the bar, making herself a drink, when she saw a guy looking at her from across the room. Their eyes met and there was instant chemistry. Like prickly heat. Within minutes, he was by her side, introducing himself. Name: Jeremy. Occupation: filmmaker.

Jeremy spent the rest of the evening asking Victoria all about herself. And he actually listened to her responses. He was funny and charming, and he only had eyes for her. By the end of the night, they were making out on the fire escape.

When the party started winding down, Victoria offered to drive Jeremy home. He was impressed with her stick-shift driving skills. And for the first time in a while, Victoria felt like she had gone from the girl with no mojo to the coolest chick on the block. So instead of driving home that night, Victoria decided to spend the night at Jeremy's. He gave her a pair of pajamas and they spent the night snuggling.

ACT TWO

That Thing Called Love

Jeremy liked to say that Victoria spent the night and never left. Which was kind of true. From that moment on, without any hesitation or doubt, they were a couple. She had someone to take to dinner parties, and he had someone to share the *New York Times* crossword with. At his house she had a drawer, a key, and the left side of the bed. Victoria made the trip to New York City almost every weekend.

Unlike past boyfriends, Victoria never felt any uncertainty with Jeremy. She liked him and he liked her. And within a few short weeks, they found themselves declaring their love for each other. Victoria found herself thinking, *This is it. We're going to get married. Maybe not right this minute, but soon.* Looking back, she realizes how naive she was. She thought that because she was ready, it would naturally happen. She was in love for the first time since college, and getting married seemed to be what adults were supposed to do. She was an adult. So, why not? Not to mention that her parents would make fatalistic comments such as, "You better hurry up and have kids. We're not going to be around forever." Like Victoria needed that pressure too.

ACT THREE
You Can Lead a Horse to Water . . .

Victoria can't quite remember how the subject of marriage first came up. But once it did, it was like a cancer. The idea of marriage seemed to invade all of their conversations and became the leading cause of all of their fights. The problem was this: Victoria wanted to get married and Jeremy didn't. Not that one day he wouldn't want to marry Victoria; he loved her deeply. It was that he couldn't see himself marrying anyone until he was in a certain place in his career.

When Victoria shared this with her father, his response was, "Then change jobs." It stood to reason that if Jeremy loved his daughter, then he should marry her. What did his career have to do with it? As far as her father was concerned, they were talking about two different things. You can't wait for your life to be perfect, for all the pieces to be in place in order

Jessica Kaminsky

to build a life together. Life doesn't work like that. Didn't it mean something that Victoria believed in Jeremy and knew that one day he would be a top director and their relationship would then fall into place? Unfortunately, it didn't. And so after many months of discussions, fights, and more fights, they decided to call it quits.

THE VERDICT

Victoria thought she could reason with Jeremy, change his opinion. But she couldn't. He didn't want to alter a single thing. He was content with the way things were. And looking back, she realizes that it was the only way their relationship could have existed. They had been confined to a schedule: She would come in on the weekends and then leave again on Sunday. And for three years, it had stayed that way.

Victoria didn't realize it at the time, but they were stuck. Jeremy just couldn't be what she wanted him to be. So when they finally ended it, she felt relieved. She had been trying to make something broken work for so long, it had exhausted her. For the first time in a long time, she felt free. And she liked it.

Rock Talk: Let's Break It Down

✳ Avoiding his phone calls, nonstop arguing, pretending to work late when you're really hanging out with your friends—these are red flags. If you're not happy, do something about it.

✳ It's hard to know when to walk away. But try to do it before the cheating begins.

✳ A good relationship cannot be built on tension and tears.

✳ If *all* you do is fight, there may be a good reason for that. It's simple . . . you're not right for each other.

✳ Ditch the dude with the issues. Jealous control freak? Good-bye. Social anxiety disorder? See ya! Your friends hate him? Sayonara.

✳ Don't be afraid to pull the plug. It's better to be yourself than one half of the non-dynamic duo.

✳ Stop being passive. Take charge of your life.

Jessica Kaminsky

BLINDED BY THE ROCK

THERE ARE TIMES IN OUR LIVES WHEN WE BECOME totally fixated on one thing. Whether it's getting that promotion at work or getting engaged, we spend so much energy conjuring, imagining, stressing about how and when this event will occur that we lose sight of *why* we want it to happen in the first place. In the case of our relationships, we often forget to ask ourselves if this is really the right person for me. Why do I want to be married so badly? And wasn't I about to break up with this guy because—oh-yeah-it-almost-slipped-my-mind— I'm *not* in love with him?

And yet when we want something (i.e., security, company, a diamond ring, a lovely house, a chance to prove our parents wrong), we ignore all logic and instead find ourselves hanging in there way past the expiration date. It's an unfortunate reality, and not everyone is eager to admit that they've stayed with someone longer than they should have for questionable reasons. But it's the truth.

The scary thing is that we often barrel ahead in our relationships without heeding the warning signs because, subconsciously, we don't want to be left behind by our peers. Whether you realize it or not, friends have an uncanny ability to influence the decisions you make—even as adults, we're not immune to peer pressure. Only now the pressure comes from within. Entirely unaware that we're doing it, we use our friends as barometers to measure our progress—both our successes and our failures.

I'll come clean. This phenomenon of being motivated for the wrong reasons has gripped me several times. I can remember the first time I felt that pang of jealousy, that gnawing sensation in my gut, that competitive tug that made me question whether or not I was falling behind. It was right after college and

I was working as an editorial assistant at a prestigious magazine, a coveted job that I barely dragged my ass out of bed to get to on time. I was working long hours and spending even longer hours in bars drinking with my friends. I was burning the candle at both ends, and yet I couldn't have been happier. Life was good, uncomplicated, and deliciously sloppy.

As for the romantic aspect, I was at the tail end of a college relationship, semi-deluding myself that we were meant to be together but really knowing in my heart that all I wanted was to be free. And yet when I heard that my friend Simone had gotten engaged, I thought to myself, "Wouldn't it be amazing if Leo (my now-ex) proposed?" Then I followed that ludicrous thought up with this one: "We'd have the most beautiful kids." As if that were somehow my life's goal.

The news of Simone's engagement was no big surprise. She had been dating her boyfriend since high school. I know what you're thinking—high school sweethearts? But Simone and Jeff were cool, artsy, and punk rock. So if they were willing to stand up in front of a room full of friends and estranged relatives and declare their unequivocal love for each other, then anyone could. Hell, *I* could.

THE TRUTH BEHIND THE ROCK

At first I was shocked that someone our age could get married—I mean I knew it technically *could* happen, but at twenty-two, she was the first to get engaged. And the news of her impending wedlock sent me into a tizzy, which is strange considering I had no prior interest in marriage. I still felt like a kid (although maybe that had something to do with the fact that I was still borrowing money from my parents on a regular basis). And yet somehow upon hearing that Simone would be walking down the aisle, I felt a profound and immediate jolt of panic.

This was my first exposure to diamond envy.

All of a sudden I had this feeling that I had fallen behind. I'd spent all those wasted hours hanging out with drunken deadbeats when, apparently, I should have been luring, convincing, and cajoling an innocent man into marrying me. And so I hatched a plan. I decided to refocus my efforts, be kind instead of cruel, and try to get my then-boyfriend to propose. Sure we had our problems—among them the fact that I could barely stand to look at him and lately I'd been pretending to work late just to avoid seeing him. But maybe if we just got engaged, our problems would go away.

Thankfully, I didn't act on my insanity. Nonetheless,

the desire for a ring from a boyfriend I was on the verge of dumping was evidence of the intense effect that the idea of wearing diamonds had on me . . . and the embarrassing lengths to which I would go to get what I thought I wanted.

More Excuses

So often, we construct elaborate reasons why we should stay with the very person we know we're not in love with. Such excuses as "think how much we'll save in rent" and "he's been so good to me, I can't just go and break his heart" may have sounded reasonable at the time. But two years later, not only do those rationalizations come off as reckless and transparent, they're crazy.

Keeping the charade of a relationship going because we're too chicken to admit that it's over, we dread confrontation, or we're too damn afraid to be alone, just prolongs the inevitable. The longer you wait to let go, the more painful it is for everyone involved. Here are some of the excuses people cling to before coming to their senses.

93

"But he's perfect on paper."

On paper, Topher was Dara's dream guy. He was a handsome, independently wealthy, warm, and generous artist. His mom was friends with her mom and the two of them just loved the fact that their children were dating. So right from the beginning, Topher was an easy choice. The infrastructure of support was in place. No need for that awkward first meeting, because her mom already knew him and loved him, which was a huge relief.

Looking back, however, she knew that there wasn't really a spark. But she thought, "I'll grow to love him." (First red flag.) They just made so much sense as a couple. Not to mention, she couldn't help liking that he took care of her. He paid for all of their meals and all of their trips. And again, it was easy to be with him. (Second red flag—you should never seriously date someone simply because it's easy.) But after a while, she realized that none of this made her happy and she began to feel very claustrophobic in his huge loft, in his sprawling country house, and in his giant ski condo. Perfect on paper doesn't always mean perfect fit.

Jessica Kaminsky

"How will he live without me?"

Now that she has a little distance, Rachel can admit that one of the reasons she stayed with Ted for as long as she did was because she "didn't want to hurt his feelings." He put her on a pedestal, which at first she loved, then grew to hate. He spoiled her, treated her like a queen. Again which she loved, then hated. *Get a spine, get some opinions of your own, stop staring at me all the time,* she found herself thinking. But she enjoyed the time that she spent with him (his saving grace was his sense of humor) and kept hoping that the love would one day "kick in." (Note: This is not a good sign. You should not have to wait for anything to "kick in" in a relationship.)

But ultimately she found the idea of breaking up with him heart wrenching. She was racked with guilt over the thought of hurting his feelings. Her anxiety over whether or not to leave him was not helped by Ted's frequent declarations that he couldn't imagine his life without her, that he felt so lucky to have finally met his soul mate, and that he couldn't wait to start a family with her. Looking back, Rachel realizes that she should have said something much earlier on, but it was hard. He seemed so helpless. Whether it was remembering to fix himself something to eat or not being able to open a bottle of champagne without her, Rachel felt like she always had to be there to hold his hand. Literally.

And that's when she realized it was all an act. Ted knew how to take care of himself. He had been doing just fine on his own for ten years. And Rachel wasn't looking to be someone's mommy, especially not her boyfriend's. At last, she had answered her own question. How will he live without me? He'll do just fine on his own.

"Think how much we'll save in rent."

Marin knew it was a bad idea right from the beginning. But when her boyfriend of six months, Zach, whispered those practical words in her ear—"Think how much we'll save in rent"—there was no way she could say no. In all of her years of dating, no one had ever asked her to move in before. It was one thing to be given a set of keys to his apartment. Sure, that felt special. But to be asked to cohabitate—now that was a newsworthy event.

Jessica Kaminsky

She was giddy with delight, her mind swirling with questions. Did she know what this meant? He loved her! He wanted to buy furniture together! And best of all, he wanted to save money with her . . . for their future! Of course the one thing she hadn't considered when she accepted his offer to move in and save money with him was whether or not she really wanted to live with him. She was so swept up in his asking that she forgot to check in with herself. And suddenly, now that all of their possessions were mingling, Marin was pretty sure she had made a huge mistake.

This rent-saving scenario has motivated many a couple to prematurely jump into living together. Think of it this way—the amount of money you think you'll save will be made up in therapy bills and the cost of getting movers to carry your belongings back to your old place. So think very carefully about this decision. Because I promise that the process of extracting yourself from a dying relationship is made doubly painful with the addition of a bitter, sad, sulking ex lurking in the corner. So until you're sure that he's the one, don't move in together. And be grateful that you have a place to escape to when things get rocky.

Rock Goggling

Have you ever experienced that sharp pang of jealousy when admiring someone's oversize diamond ring? Either the purely superficial variety: "I love that ring. I want that ring." Or the more competitive kind: "I love that ring. Why does she get that ring?" Welcome to Rock Goggling. It's like "beer goggling," only replace the alcohol with the sparkly, shiny effects of diamonds. This phenomenon has caused women to act irrationally and say things they otherwise would never express out loud. Take Carrie, for instance. When her best friend, Joelle, got engaged, Carrie immediately went over to congratulate her and admire her friend's new sparkler. But when she saw the enormity of the ring, she was rendered speechless. And then later, when Carrie and her boyfriend went to look at engagement rings, she skipped right past the single stones and went straight for the three-stone setting, explaining that the "smaller" rings made her hand look fat.

Rock Goggling is powerful and must therefore be monitored, and a Rock Goggler is not to be trusted. She cannot be held responsible for her actions.

Jessica Kaminsky

Straight from the Horse's Mouth

If you've got a guy who just stares at the ground, playing with some imaginary dirt, every time you want answers, Kevin is here to shed some light on the subject of engagement pressure.

What was your reaction to the news that your girlfriend Amy's best friend had gotten engaged?

I had two reactions. First, I was absolutely thrilled for her friend. They're a great couple. And my second reaction was, "Crap, we're going to have to have another talk about marriage." It always went down the same way. Whenever she'd tell me about someone who had gotten engaged, the subtext was: And why aren't we engaged yet? It was as if it didn't matter that we weren't ready or that we might be on the verge of breaking up. At times, it didn't even seem to matter if it was me who did the asking. She just wanted to be proposed to and if I were smart, I had better do it soon.

But I loved her and saw how much angst this was causing her. So I did us both a favor and proposed. Besides, if I hadn't, I'm pretty sure her head would have exploded.

SOME ENGAGING HISTORY

* The largest uncut diamond ever found was the Cullinan in South Africa circa 1905, coming in at 3,106 carats.

* Rocker Chris Robinson proposed to his wife, actress Kate Hudson, with an old-fashioned 5-carat Asscher-cut diamond in an art deco setting.

* The King of Rock and Roll, Elvis Presley, proposed to his then-girlfriend, Priscilla Beaulieu, with a 3.5-carat diamond ring surrounded by an additional row of detachable diamonds.

He Said/She Said

Introducing the now defunct . . .

Greg & Karen

Greg and Karen dated for a year and a half. Which, Greg believes, is exactly the amount of time you can be in a relationship before the issue of marriage comes up. This is their story.

Jessica Kaminsky

ACT ONE

I Have the Perfect Guy for You

She said: Karen worked in a fancy Beverly Hills salon as a hairdresser. All day, ladies of leisure would sit in her chair and tell her stories about their husbands, the trips they planned on taking, and the newest restaurants to go to while she cut and trimmed their elaborately coiffed dos. So when one of them offered to set her up with someone, Karen leaped at the chance.

He said: Greg has always considered himself a frugal guy. And even though he makes a fair amount of money working in film, he has always taken great pride in driving the crappiest car amongst his friends, an ancient Mazda he bought for $700. And *that* was the car he picked Karen up in.

She said: Karen was expecting someone very different. When she heard that Greg wrote feature films, she envisioned a slick guy in a beamer. Not someone who wore ripped T-shirts and drove a car that frequently stalled out at stop signs. She wasn't a total snob, though. She had grown up with nothing, living in a trailer park with her mom. But she was dead set on finding a financially successful man to share her life with. No more double-wides for her.

While it seemed like these two would never make it past their first date, they had great chemistry. So they continued to date.

ACT TWO
Opposites Attract

Even though Greg and Karen were an unlikely couple (she cared about appearances while Greg considered it a point of pride that he would never own a suit), they still enjoyed each other's company and connected on a deeper level. But as they became more serious about each other, Karen's issues with Greg began to bubble to the surface. And one night while visiting a coworker of Greg's at his gorgeous midcentury home tucked in the Hollywood Hills, Karen expressed her concerns. If they were going to build a future together, she needed more security.

Since she was never going to see Greg (due to the long hours he worked) *and* she wasn't going to have the nice house, what was in it for her? As far as she could tell, it was a lose-lose situation. Greg couldn't believe that Karen could be so superficial. Didn't she under-

Jessica Kaminsky

stand that he was saving his money so that one day he could own an even nicer house than she was envisioning? But she considered his thrifty ways selfish, not prudent. And to make matters more complicated, she wanted a ring on her finger and she wanted it soon.

ACT THREE

Now or Never

Greg was feeling intense pressure from Karen to get engaged. The way she saw it, they had been together for a year and a half and she wanted a commitment. Meanwhile, Greg was trying to figure out some things himself, particularly whether or not this appearances-obsessed woman was the person he wanted to spend the rest of his life with. He was thinking not, but before he could come to a conclusion, Karen gave Greg an ultimatum. She wanted to get engaged and she wanted it to happen by her birthday in September. It was May, which bought Greg a few months. This would have been okay—awkward, but okay—except that Karen threw another wrench into the equation. She decided to stop having sex with him until she got the ring. So they compromised and agreed to go to couples' therapy.

Couples' therapy was a nightmare. The therapist asked Greg point blank why he wouldn't marry Karen. He felt put on the spot and pinned down. So he canceled the next appointment. When Karen learned what he had done, she lost it and had a screaming breakdown on the street. Didn't he realize what a treasure she was? Why couldn't he move forward? He was never going to amount to anything! He was a loser! That was it, it was over! She stormed off into the night. And true to her word, that was it. By the time Greg got home, Karen had packed up the contents of her drawer and gathered the few possessions she had kept at his house. Greg felt like he had been the star of an episode of *The Young and the Restless*.

By the time his relationship with Karen ended, Greg had gotten so used to the fighting, the yelling, and the drama of it all that he had almost forgotten that they *could* end it. They didn't have to stay together. Duh. It seemed so obvious, and yet it had been so hard to see his way out. So when Karen got fed up and declared their relationship over, he was relieved. Very relieved.

THE VERDICT

Greg is now married to an amazing woman who shares his love of thriftiness and junky cars, while Karen married a banker and finally got that big house she always dreamed of. In this case, opposites did not attract.

Rock Talk: Let's Break It Down

* Just because your friend got engaged doesn't mean you have to too. Repeat after me: It is *not* a race.

* You're miserable. You can barely stand to hear the sound of his voice. You daydream about freak accidents that might befall him and thus free you from the relationship once and for all. Guess what? It's time to break up.

* Perfect on paper means just that—he's perfect on paper. You want perfect in *person*.

* No matter how much money you may save by living with your boyfriend, do not move in together unless you envision a future with him beyond next week.

✴ Remember, this is your life, not your parents'. They don't have to sleep with the brilliant but boring guy who has won their approval—you do. So ditch the stiff.

✴ You can get a diamond from anyone. Hell, you can even buy one yourself. So don't settle just because you think you should be engaged.

PART TWO:
AFTER THE ROCK

6

SHOW ME THE ROCK

SO HERE YOU ARE, POSITIVELY GLOWING AFTER an amazing weekend. Why was it so amazing? Well, for one, YOU GOT ENGAGED! That's right. You, the girl who was sure she would die alone in a pile of her own filth surrounded by cats, got engaged. Someone wants to spend the rest of his life with you. YOU! And to all those naysayers who passed silent judgment and told you he couldn't commit, you say, "Ha! Take that, bitches!" 'Cause now you've got something sparkly on your finger to prove them wrong. That's right. You are a closer, my friend. *You* get things done. Although, technically, you weren't the one who did the "proposing." No matter, because where would he be without your subtle yet pointed needling and around-the-clock hinting? Nowhere, that's where. He asked you to marry him and you said yes. So if you need to shout it out one more time, go ahead. You've earned it. You're *engaged*!

Now that the dust has settled and the calls to friends have been made, it's time to resume your life. Which means that come Monday, chances are you'll be heading back to work. And while you may be feeling bummed out that your magical weekend of romance has come to an end, try looking at it this way—at long last, you finally have something to talk about with your coworkers. No more rifling in the dark for Monday-morning conversation, because you've got the winning ticket. You got engaged. And people *love* engagements. It sounds trite, but it's true. People adore engagements just as much as they love puppies with big floppy ears and snapshots of babies propped up on their chubby arms.

Engagements represent the start of a beautiful life together. Not only that, but people never tire of clucking and cooing over a newly acquired gem. And they want to know *everything*. How it happened, what time of day he asked and where, who knew beforehand, whether or not he picked out the ring by himself—no detail is too mundane. Whether it's your office buddy or that woman whose name you can never remember in human resources, they all want to bask in the warmth of your news. So get ready . . . come Monday, you're going to be the toast of the watercooler.

This can be both thrilling and utterly exhausting. The fun part comes in the beginning when you get to tell people all of the thoughtful little things your guy came up with—the diversionary tactics, the phony dinner reservations to throw you off the scent, and the weeks he spent nervously carrying the ring in his pocket, transferring it from one pair of pants to the next, all the while trying to choose that perfect moment to propose. Then, of course, there's the actual engagement. What he said to you and where he chose to ask. All of these elements will be permanently etched in your memory, and it's exciting to share them with friends or, really, anyone who'll listen.

But eventually, and trust me on this, you *will* become bored by your own engagement story. It may be the most interesting, beautifully orchestrated, thrilling proposal ever delivered, but after a few solid days of recounting it over and over again, you'll

Jessica Kaminsky

discover that the mere thought of having to repeat it one more time is enough to drive even the most social person into self-imposed isolation. You'll wish that you had had the foresight to tape-record yourself back in the beginning (when you still sounded believably enthusiastic); that way you could just hit play and take a quick snooze while Judy in accounting gets up to speed on your love life.

The night Dave and I got engaged we were getting ready for an evening of parties and excessive drinking. It was New Year's Eve and we were about to head out the door when Dave asked me if I'd like to take a walk with him. It was an unusual request, given that we were in New York City in the middle of winter, but I obliged, sensing that maybe, just maybe, he had a plan. So there we were taking a casual stroll in the bitter cold, when I realized that Dave was steering us toward Central Park. Now, most New Yorkers know that when the sun goes down you don't enter the park for fear of being mugged by gangs of marauding teenagers or weird perverts ready to strike at any turn. But I didn't want to kill the mood. So I bottled up my paranoia and decided to just roll with it.

We continued our journey into the depths of the park, walking and talking for what seemed like forever. Dave plopped down on a bench just as I was beginning to think that maybe he was simply trying to escape from my family, which was in town visiting. But when I sat down and turned to face him, he seemed nervous, twitchy, and preoccupied. Actually, his behavior was not all that different from the man chatting with his Styrofoam cup by the garbage can.

And that's when it really hit me. . . . Oh my God, it's about to happen. Dave is going to propose to me. *Wait, wait, wait,* I thought, as I ran through my mental checklist. How was my breath? Too cold to tell. Hair? Frozen solid under a wool hat. And why, oh why, didn't I put on my makeup before we left? So I did the only thing I could think of—I took off my hat and gave the best *Charlie's Angels* hair shake I could muster. Sure, it was cold and my ears felt like ice chips, but I was going to look good, damn it. At last, I was ready.

Dave was sort of half on the bench, half in a semi-kneel—the subzero version of getting down on bended knee. He told me that he had been giving it a lot of thought and that he hoped I knew how much

Jessica Kaminsky

he loved me. (I did.) And that he couldn't imagine a life without me. (I felt the same way.) Then he asked me if I'd marry him. In my mind, I said yes, yes, YES! But in reality, I started laughing. First it was a little giggle. Then it grew into a deep belly laugh with a couple of snorts tossed into the mix. It was a happy laugh, mind you—a semidelirious "I can't believe I'm getting married" laugh.

But the fact remained I hadn't given Dave an answer. And he really didn't seem to be enjoying my irrepressible bout of giggles. He looked at me, nervously. "Well, what's your answer?"

"Yes, yes!" I said, and kissed him. "Of course, yes."

Then he reached into his pocket and took out a small box. Inside was this gorgeous ring. Tasteful, elegant, perfect. I slipped it on and it was an exact fit. Dave looked proud. Then I suddenly remembered that we were in the park after dark with a sketchy man lurking nearby, so I grabbed Dave's hand and we bolted.

The rest of that night was a giddy blur. We ran back to the apartment, burst in the door, and yelled, "We got engaged!" My parents were thrilled. We then went out to meet some friends. On the way to the party, I kept staring down at the twinkly bauble now occupying my ring finger. I couldn't believe it. I was a girl with a ring. Me. It seemed so strange, so foreign. The very thing I had pushed for all this time was actually here . . . on my finger, in fact.

On the one hand, I felt like an imposter. I rarely ever wore jewelry. I think I've worn the same earrings for approximately ten years. And now I was a girl with a diamond. Where was my matching sweater set and perfectly coiffed mane? And yet, on the other hand, my beautiful engagement ring had suddenly transformed my hand into something elegant and feminine. I barely recognized it. Historically, my hands have always been pretty unremarkable. They're kind of pudgy with chubby little fingers. Long nails make them look like the hands of a trannie. Basically, they're peasantlike, meant for a life of pulling potatoes out of the ground and making hearty stews. But now, here was my left hand, riding the L train, decked out in a sparkly diamond. It was odd. And yet, somehow right. As I stared down at my hand with its new diamond, I thought, "I like you. You're pretty."

When we walked into the party, I remember again shouting, "We got engaged!" (Apparently, I had one line and I was sticking to it.) Immediately there was a swirl of activity around us—hugging, kissing, a lot of handshaking and backslapping for Dave, and the sound of clinking glasses. Cheers abounded. But after that, Dave and I barely saw each other the rest of the night. We both got swept off into huddles divided by sex. Dave was with a group of guys, sharing tips on how he got the diamond (all I could hear was something about how you had to know a *"guy."*), while I was with the ladies telling the proposal story and passing around the ring for friends to admire and try on. We only briefly rejoined at the stroke of midnight to kiss, and then it was back to our respective corners.

During the course of that night, I think I must have told at least twenty people about how we got engaged. I regaled them with the backstory, the real story, the story behind the story, and then I got on the phone with friends in Los Angeles and did it all over again. I talked so much that when I woke up the next morning, my head didn't hurt from too much champagne, my jaw hurt from gabbing. Not only did I want to take a three-day recuperative vow of silence, but I never wanted to tell the story of how we got engaged again. I was talked out.

However, I knew that somehow a curt version would come off as hostile, ungrateful, troubled. I love Dave with all my heart, and yet if I never had to tell anyone the story of how we got engaged again, I'd die happy. And so I concocted a plan. I'd lie.

I know that sounds awful, lying about your engagement. But it wasn't so much lying as avoiding. I just couldn't stand the thought of telling it one more time. So I developed two approaches. One was the "I'm running out the door and can't talk" tactic. I'd explain that five minutes couldn't do the story justice and ask if we could save it for the next time we talked. People always understood.

My second tactic to avoid sharing the story simply involved telling a seriously edited version of what happened. For instance, I'd say, "We got engaged on New Year's Eve in Central Park. It was simple, straightforward, to the point. Just like Dave." In general, people found this version unsatisfying. I could see it in their eyes. They wanted to hear everything, right down to my goofy giggle fit. They wanted it all. But I was tired. Couldn't they see that?

The point is, every engagement is unique in its own way. Special, simple, elaborate—however it happened,

Jessica Kaminsky

it's yours. Now you may be one of the lucky ones, possibly thanks to a chatty mother, sister, or best friend who passes the story along for you, who doesn't have to repeat the story until your gums bleed and you grow to hate it. Or you may be the kind of freakish person who never tires of your tale. But either way, you're engaged now. Which means that people will paw at you, comment on your ring, and share their personal thoughts on marriage with you whether you like it or not. The floodgates have been opened.

The Diamond Ambush

Ah, the diamond ambush. This is the period of time that stretches from the day you get engaged until that moment you walk down the aisle. You will be on the receiving end of people (ranging from close friends to virtual strangers) lunging for your newly bejeweled hand, eager to know every detail of how your guy popped the question. People will want to know the history of your new bauble and where he bought it. (Translation: How much did that thing cost?) And like it or not, folks will make comments and share their anxieties about their own futures.

Who knew that simply sporting a ring made you a relationship expert? In the eyes of many, your shiny sparkler is a testament to your ability to lock down a mate, however arcane and old-fashioned that sounds. In the eyes of many, you are the lucky one. So get ready for the diamond ambush, because it's open season in crazy town. Here are a few things to watch out for in particular:

The Grabber

When you tell people that you got engaged, don't be surprised when they grab your hand to get a gander at your ring. They'll admire it, comment on its size, remark on its shape—they may even ask to try it on. Or you may surprise yourself by volunteering to slip it off for anyone interested in giving it a test drive. How else can you fill the awkward silence as someone stares speechlessly at your hand? Now, none of this is a problem if you're showing your ring to friends. That's great. But if the attention being heaped in your direction is coming from a nosy coworker or your busybody neighbor, that's when it might start to feel overbearing and intrusive.

So when it comes to that irritating person who just doesn't know how to stop the touching and refuses to read the signs, my advice is to cover your mouth and fake a cough. Then as you extend your hand to let them examine the ring, warn them not to get too close—this persistent cold you have is a doozy; you wouldn't want them to catch it. Feel free to do whatever it takes to drive your point home so that you can be left in peace.

The Gabber

This is that person who just loves to chew your ear off about engagements. They'll chat with you about friends who are in the throes of wedding-planning hell, or celebrity couples they've read about. They might even toss in a little bit of their own premarital experiences. But the most distinctive quality about the Gabber is their unique ability to never shut up due to a false assumption on their part that simply because you're engaged, you care to hear about other people's experiences. It's the same thing with babies. If you have one, everyone assumes you love all babies. Not true. You love your baby, just as you love your ring and your soon-to-be spouse. This doesn't mean you have to care about anyone else's stories. So nod politely, then make an excuse and bolt for the door. Don't worry about the Gabber. They'll find someone else to bore to death.

Know your stats.

While it's true that people are clamoring to hear your engagement story, they are also dying to know those cold hard diamond facts. From shape to size, cut to clarity, platinum to white gold. No diamond detail is too small. They want it all. They're information sponges. And why are they so curious about your preference for an emerald cut over a round-shaped diamond? Because they're fishing around for themselves, silly. They're trying to imagine what they'd like to wear on their hand. Or they're trying to gauge if their boyfriend would ever be capable of pulling off such a purchase on his own.

So are you wearing a princess cut on a platinum band? Or do you have a radiant setting with baguettes? You need to know your diamond: Know how many carats you're sporting, know where your guy made his purchase, and know how he chose the place. Did someone help him pick it out? And if so, who? Your single friends will want to know about the advance planning and all the details so that they can then go home and poke around like bomb-sniffing dogs. Now aren't you glad you're on the other side?

Jessica Kaminsky

Ringless in Seattle

What happens when you get engaged and you don't have a ring? Well, obviously, nothing "happens." People get engaged all the time without an actual ring. The ring is, after all, just a symbol. And maybe you're not into symbols. Or perhaps your guy wanted you to be there when he picked out the ring because the last piece of jewelry he bought for you currently lives in the bottom of a shoe box, next to some feather earrings from when you were a kid. Whatever the reason may be, if you are engaged and are not sporting some kind proof, it can be, well . . . awkward.

Whenever news of an engagement is announced, people's eyes instinctively float down to your left hand like a dirty old man uncontrollably staring at a woman's chest. So you can either explain why you don't have a ring on: You don't believe in them. You find engagements rings too flashy. Your boyfriend is currently trying to finance a trip to the jewelers. The ring is getting resized. Or you can let that person squirm in discomfort as they try to recover from having been caught peeking at your ringless finger. Disappointed? Deal with it.

Oh my God, it's HUGE.

Every once in a while a close friend will get engaged and when everyone gathers around to check out her shiny new ring, there's always one person in the group who can't help but exclaim the obvious: "Jesus, woman. How much does that thing weigh?" People's rings seem to be getting bigger and bigger. Whether it's granny's ring from the old country, or just an old-fashioned giant diamond, it seems that ladies every-where are sporting diamonds that could double as hand weights. Are two carats the new one carat? Just remember—bigger isn't always better.

It's not the size that counts.

Just as a giant ring will attract attention in the form of unsolicited comments ("It's enormous!" Translation: "How tacky!"), a more modest ring may also invite a similar stream of remarks ("It's adorable!" Transla-tion: "Mine is bigger"). Women are always compar-ing, contrasting, dissecting. Where do they fit in? And how does their ring compare? They feel reassured by the sight of a smaller ring. Or they feel uncomfortable in the presence of an obscenely large one.

Jessica Kaminsky

Just as men (both consciously and subconsciously) compare their penis size with that of the guy standing next to them at the urinal, women do the same with their diamonds. And while you may not be this kind of person, you probably know someone who is. She's the one who dove for your hand, then called your ring "sweet" (Translation: "small"). But who cares what she thinks? You love it. It's yours. So try not to let the ring-Nazis bother you, because in this case, size does not matter.

Straight from the Horse's Mouth

Picking out a ring has to be the most daunting task for a boyfriend on the verge of proposing. Not only is he dropping an obscene amount of cash, but what if he gets it wrong and she doesn't like it? Eric gives his take on the process of purchasing a breathtakingly beautiful ring that won't break the bank but will satisfy all of her hopes and dreams.

Were you nervous buying your then-girlfriend an engagement ring? Had she given you an idea of what she might want?

Nervous doesn't even begin to capture it. More like totally freaked out. Why do you think I put it off for so long? And it wasn't just about whether she'd like it or not. There were other factors to consider. Like, how much was I supposed to spend? How much could I afford to spend? And how little could I get away with spending without appearing to be a total cheapskate? After all, I did want her to say yes.

So I began by doing some research. The one thing I started to hear about, before I had even considered what my budget might be, was the Two-Month Rule. The Two-Month Rule suggests that however much you make over a two-month period is the amount you can afford to spend on a ring. Now that's all fine and dandy when you have a regular day job, but when you're a freelance writer that sum can vary tremendously. For instance, I made plenty of money this month. But last month, I dined mainly on Ramen noodles. So to get a real sense of my budget, I unearthed my tax returns, divided my annual income over twelve months, and figured out what my monthly salary would be. That is, if I actually had a monthly salary. And then I took it from there.

Once I knew how much I could technically afford, I felt a little better. I then enlisted her best friend and we set out in search of something shiny. I did have some sense of what I was looking for. My lady has always loved antiques and her favorite jewelry is this pair of earrings she inherited from her grandmother. So I knew that I wasn't going to get her some brand-spanking-new diamond. Anyway the whole thing took time. I visited many different jewelers, and I told a lot of lies to distract her from my frequent excursions.

In the end, I settled on a ruby stone, which is her birthstone (my idea, thank you very much), surrounded by a ring of tiny diamonds in a platinum band. I never worried that she wouldn't like it or might be disappointed. Thankfully I never heaped that head trip on myself. And I guess I thought it was beautiful, so I felt she would too. In the end, it was a real growth experience. I learned lots of new terms. Before I might have thought the Four Cs were a band. Now I know it's carat, cut, clarity, and color. Check me out.

THE TRUTH BEHIND THE ROCK

*"My mother says I didn't open my eyes
for eight days after I was born, but when I did,
the first thing I saw was an engagement ring.
I was hooked."* —Elizabeth Taylor

SOME ENGAGING HISTORY

* Elizabeth Taylor's fifth husband (Richard Burton)
  gave her a sixty-nine-carat diamond ring. It was later
  renamed the Burton-Taylor Diamond by Cartier.

* Taylor's fourth husband, Eddie Fisher, said that a
  $50,000 diamond could only keep her happy for
  approximately four days.

* Colored diamonds come in every shade of the
  rainbow and are both rare and very expensive.
  Yellow diamonds, for example, are colored by the
  naturally occurring addition of nitrogen, while pink
  diamonds achieve their unique color by simply
  reflecting light differently from white diamonds.

* A two-carat diamond is worth more than twice as
  much as two one-carat diamonds.

Jessica Kaminsky

He Said/She Said

A real-life couple shares what brought them together and made their relationship work.

Sasha & Oliver

They started dating in the summer of 2003. Two years later, they got engaged in Ireland. This is their story.

She said: When Sasha first started seeing Oliver, she immediately categorized it as a fling. First off, he was too good looking; he could have been a model. And then there was his body. He looked like he spent entire days at the gym. Plus, Sasha had recently been burned by love and was feeling reserved when it came to the idea of becoming emotionally invested in a new relationship. She just wasn't sure she had it in her to go through the act of falling in love and getting hurt again so soon. And yet there was a part of her that knew that she'd never find someone without making an effort.

He said: Oliver met Sasha through a mutual friend at work. First they flirted casually in the cafeteria over turkey sandwiches, and then later at a soccer game.

Although he barely knew her and they had only talked a handful of times, in no time he was totally smitten. Sasha was entirely different from the other girls he had dated. She was smart and sexy, funny yet self-deprecating, and confident with a touch of insecurity. And they had great chemistry; every time he was around her he would get all warm and tingly.

But he could tell that she didn't take him seriously. It was as if she was looking through him, not at him. But he felt like if he just hung in there, she'd come around. So he was persistent but not pushy. And after several months, Oliver's patience paid off.

ACT ONE

Before the Rock

She said: Sasha remembers the moment when she fell for Oliver. They had been dating exclusively for a while, but she still had reservations. She hadn't opened herself entirely to the relationship yet.

One night they went to a party and as things were winding down, Sasha went to get her coat in the back room. Oliver came with her. The room was filled with piles of jackets, bags, and scarves. Her blazer was nowhere in sight. Just when she was thinking, *Crap, I'm never going to find it,* Oliver, knee deep in coats, pulled it out of the pile. He looked triumphant.

Sasha thanked him for finding her blazer, and he looked at her seriously and said he would do anything for her. And just like that, her heart melted. She knew she was in love. She told him that she loved him. He said that he had loved her for a long time. They fell onto the bed, making out. Only later did she find out that this intensely private, passionate moment had in fact been totally public. They were upstairs in a room overlooking the garden where the majority of the guests were hanging out. And unbeknownst to them, their kiss had been illuminated for all to see. But she was too happy to be embarrassed.

He said: Once Oliver and Sasha decided to move in together, he felt that marriage was inevitable. The idea had been percolating for a while on a subconscious level. But once he started to pack up his belongings, he quickly found himself dividing his possessions into two piles. One pile comprised things that would make the move to their new home, and the other was items that he felt he had outgrown—

the requisite college futon, fluorescent lamp, and beanbag chair. It was the simple act of shedding these possessions that he had dutifully carried with him for so many years that made Oliver realize he was ready to take the next step. He was ready to ask Sasha to marry him.

She said: Sasha wanted Oliver to move in . . . in theory. But she needed to be 100 percent comfortable with the idea, and she wasn't quite there yet. Also, she needed Oliver to know that she didn't want him to move in unless they were going to get engaged. She couldn't bear the thought of living together with someone, breaking up, and then having to go through the process of untangling their possessions. So when Oliver assured her that he envisioned a life with her, she agreed to let him move in with her. But there was still a little part of her that felt nervous.

She wasn't looking for a roommate. And she didn't want the fact that they were moving in together to delay the prospect of getting engaged. But what could she do? She had to take that leap of faith.

He said: They had been living together for a few months when Oliver went down to Washington, D.C., for a wedding shower. He was sitting in a bar with an old friend, telling him about the recent move and his upcoming trip to Ireland with Sasha. He had lived there for a year and couldn't wait to spend time with her in a place that was so special to him. And just like that, he found himself saying, "What if I proposed to Sasha in Ireland?" And so a plan was hatched.

She said: Sasha knew the engagement might happen soon-ish. She had made it clear enough that she wanted to be engaged by the end of the year. But she wasn't expecting it to happen on their trip that summer. Oliver had asked her several times for her help picking out a ring, but she found herself ignoring his request. She didn't know what she wanted, and the whole idea of going to a jewelry shop, pointing to a pricey gem, and saying, "That one, please," then expecting her boyfriend to return and buy it made her feel uncomfortable.

ACT TWO

The Proposal

He said: The way Oliver envisioned it, a well-conceived engagement should be surprising yet inevitable. So he sought the advice of friends. He talked with one woman who told him about how her fiancé had planned an elaborate proposal, but when he actually asked her if she would marry him, he was tongue-tied. He had spent so much time and energy conceiving the scene and the build up to the engagement that he had forgotten to think about why exactly he wanted to spend his life with her and what it was about her that made him want to get married. So she impressed upon Oliver the need to really consider those questions.

She said: They had just checked into an inn on the west coast of Ireland when Oliver insisted that they drop everything and take a hike before the sun went down. Sasha was game, and soon they were walking in a gorgeous, lush green field on their way to a cliff overlooking the ocean. Sasha didn't know what to expect, but when it started to rain and Oliver showed no sign of turning back, she knew they were in for a long trek.

During their hike they were surrounded by a herd of cows, Oliver was electrocuted while trying to jump a fence, and they had to sneak past a bull standing menacingly under a tree. Sasha distinctly remembers staring up at a giant cliff and Oliver telling her that the ocean was just on the other side of the hill. But by this point she was exhausted and she just couldn't bring herself to scale the steep mountain in the rain and mud. She was ready to turn back. And that's when Oliver proposed.

He said: As Oliver began his proposal speech, he described the west coast of Ireland as one of the most beautiful places on earth. The landscape was stunning and a little bit terrifying, and he told her that everything about where they were reminded him of her. He saw their surroundings as a metaphor for how he felt about her—exciting and full of adventure. Then he asked Sasha if she would marry him. She said yes, and he took out a simple platinum band, a "promise ring." When they got back to New York, she could pick out exactly what she wanted. If there was one thing he knew, it was that Sasha liked things a certain way—her way—and that was one of the things he loved about her. He wanted her to be part of the decision on which ring she would wear for the rest of her life.

ACT THREE

Getting the Rock

She said: Even though she didn't have a rock on her finger when she got back to the States, everything about how they got engaged was perfect—even Oliver's brush with death by electrocution. And she liked the fact that she got to pick out her ring. A week after they got home, Sasha went to try on rings with her aunt and a friend. She would have felt too self-conscious if Oliver had come with her, worrying the entire time about his budget and not focusing on what she liked. Instead she felt like a princess, perusing trays of diamonds and stones. After some deliberation, she landed on a yellow diamond with sapphire baguettes on a gold band.

He said: Oliver got the call from Sasha that she had picked out the ring and that he was now supposed to go to the address she gave him, armed with his checkbook. They would laugh about it later, saying that the act of Oliver buying the ring had all the romance of dropping off a sample at the sperm bank. But Sasha couldn't be happier now that the engagement was official, and Oliver felt relieved, content, settled. It was nice to be on the other side.

Even though Sasha and Oliver are in the midst of planning their upcoming wedding, they both feel like the hard part is over. Not that they won't face the normal challenges of a married couple. It's just that after the act of getting engaged and the time it took for them to get there, they already feel as if they're married. And it feels pretty good.

Rock Talk: Let's Break It Down

✳ Put your cocktail conversation aside, because now that you're engaged, like it or not, you'll be required to talk about the proposal for months.

✳ People love engagements, so get ready to be the most popular girl in the office. Nothing unifies a staff more than discussing a rock—except maybe cake in the conference room.

✳ Not all reactions to your big news are going to be enthusiastic. So try not to take it too personally when one or both of your parents look like they're going to throw up when you tell them of your impending nuptials. They're just coming to terms with the fact that you're not their baby girl anymore.

✳ Tired of telling your engagement story for the forty-millionth time? Get creative, spice it up, tone it down, make it short and sweet.

✳ People will dive for your hand once they hear you're engaged. So brace yourself for the full-frontal assault.

7

LOCKED THE ROCK

BEFORE YOU GOT ENGAGED, IT WAS ALL ABOUT your boyfriend's progress. Specifically, when was he going to ask you to marry him and what the hell was taking so long? In other words, the onus was on him to do all the work. Well of course, he didn't do *all* the work. After all, you had to warm him up to the idea. And then it fell on your shoulders not to be offended by his frequent freak-outs. Remember when he claimed to "not believe in marriage"? Or he needed to "be in a better place in his career"? Indeed those were some frustrating times.

The good news is you both got through it. And in the end your persistence paid off. He stepped up to the plate. He bought a beautiful ring, crafted a heart-felt proposal, and did his best to surprise you. And by the way, you're not easy to surprise. You're like a bloodhound during the holiday season. And yet he managed to purchase and hold on to a ring without your ever knowing that it had crossed the threshold of your home. And then when he took you out to dinner under the guise of celebrating a promotion, you didn't see an engagement coming. So it worked. He surprised you. See, he's good for something.

So, now that the initial feeling of elation (Yes! My guy did it! He pulled it together. I never thought it was possible. Way to go, guy!) has dissipated, how do you feel? On the one hand, this is something that you've wanted for a long time. For God's sake, you even went ring shopping together! And yet, now that the dust has settled and the smoke has cleared, there is that unmistakable panicky feeling. It's like you've forgotten why you wanted to be engaged so badly in the first place.

Rest assured, you're going to be fine. You're experiencing a teeny-tiny, eensy-weensy panic attack. But don't worry. The anxiety, the voices in your head, and your sudden aversion to the color white are all *totally* normal. You've got a standard case of cold feet. In other words, you have officially entered the Valley of the Shadow of Doubt. (Cue the spooky, haunted-house sounds, please.)

Now, I'm no Dr. Phil, but in interviewing many folks for this book, one theme that kept coming up over and over again is that women tend to pursue their desire to get engaged with abandon. We covet, we drop hints, we campaign aggressively—and then after all of that time and energy has been spent getting our men to propose, we're suddenly filled with doubt. Existential doubt, identity issues, cold feet. And we have to reckon with crazy thoughts like *What was the big rush? Maybe I'm the one who doesn't believe in marriage*, and *Why wasn't I a bigger slut in my twenties?* Which is pretty interesting, considering that these were the exact same questions you had to answer for your boyfriend back when you first broached the subject of marriage. That's right, the tables have turned. It's Freaky Friday—only this time, you're the freak!

As luck would have it, just as you're coming undone, your fella (I mean . . . gulp . . . fiancé) has never seemed happier. After having cleared the engagement hurdle, the pressure is finally off. He can officially sit

THE TRUTH BEHIND THE ROCK

back, relax, switch on the autopilot, and set the ol' cruise control to a safe, comfortable speed of 50 mph. For him, the hard part was the time leading up to the engagement (everything it represented, coming to terms with the end of his life of bachelorhood, facing the future, etc.). But now that he's overcome those issues and is officially engaged, it's like a giant weight has been lifted, while you're wearing out the hall carpet with all of your nervous pacing. What gives?

Of course, we're all different and some women never go through feelings of uncertainty. However, for me, it wasn't until after I was officially engaged, ring on finger, that I was able to take my emotional temperature. I had been so focused on wanting the rock that I hadn't asked myself how it would feel once I finally got it.

After Dave and I got engaged, the whole idea of marriage started to take on surreal proportions. It was as if I'd forgotten that "getting engaged" was just one stop on the road. I'd have these moments where I'd stare down at my ring and wiggle my fingers. Yep, it was my hand all right. But it didn't feel like mine. I was literally having trouble connecting the ring on my hand to my body and my mind. Sometimes I'd just stare blankly at Dave and wonder how we ended up here. We used to be so free. Now look at us, stressing over guest lists, party favors, and whether to go with a six- or eight-piece band. Who had we become?

Luckily, although I was having this identity crisis, I wasn't unhappy. I loved Dave and couldn't wait to start our life together. It was just that all of a sudden the enormity of our decision had finally dawned on me. We were getting married, and soon we'd be exchanging rings, sharing vows, and publicly pledging to build a life together based on honesty and compassion. I believed in all of those things. So why did I suddenly feel like a pinball in a machine?

Looking back, I think that it was the first time I was truly reckoning with the intensity of growing up and the vulnerability of not knowing 100 percent how something would turn out. Yes, I loved this man. Yes, I envisioned a life with him through highs and lows. But there weren't any guarantees it would work. I mean, I had never done this before. What did I know? And how did I grow up so quickly? I swear just yesterday I was a fun-loving twentysomething.

So how did I handle these existential woes? Well, after some private meltdowns and several extended sessions with my therapist, I shared my nervousness and anxiety with Dave. He listened, nodded sagely, and then told me that he understood completely. Turns out not too many months ago he had experienced the same panicky sensation. So after he soothed my nerves and assured me that we would get through this, it was like I fell in love all over again. Do you hear that? Your biggest fears don't have to be your dirtiest secrets. So bare your souls, ladies. And let the one you love tell you it'll all be okay. Because it will.

How to Handle That Unforeseen Panic Attack (aka Be Careful What You Wish For)

If you could describe your current post-engagement state of mind, would you say you're thrilled? Ecstatic? Mind running a mile a minute, whirling with plots and dreams all involving long stem roses, soft lighting, and you wearing white and standing in front of a room full of friends and estranged relatives? Or are you suddenly paralyzed with an unshakeable fear at the thought of having to walk down the aisle?

Just as men have been known to demonstrate a distaste for the "let's get engaged" talk, women who have been focused only on getting the ring can experience a post-proposal crisis. That "Holy shit! What have I done? Who the hell is this belly-scratching, ripped-shirt-wearing, video game–playing man-child?" feeling. So if any of this sounds vaguely familiar, take heart in knowing that you are not alone.

But before you do anything rash like throwing your ring into the ocean, flirting with a complete stranger, or faking your own kidnapping, it's important to take a moment to evaluate the situation and ask yourself how deep your anxiety level runs. Is it a passing phase, or is it here to stay? Because the better you understand what you're afraid of, the easier it will be for you to communicate your concerns to your mate. Below, two women share how they handled their less-than-storybook reactions to getting engaged.

Lindsay

Lindsay had been dating Mike for close to three years when they got engaged. She was a few years older than him and had a strong sense of what she wanted. So after two years of dating, she sat Mike down and asked him point-blank if he wanted to take their relationship to the next level. She needed to know because not only did she want to get married, she was also ready to have kids.

When Lindsay thinks about how she first broached the subject with Mike, she laughs. "He must have had a complete panic attack. Not only was he getting pressure from me to propose, but he knew that when he did I wanted to get pregnant right away." Indeed, Mike was freaking out. It was the one-two punch: Getting married and having kids. Weren't they a little young to be thinking about having a family, Mike wondered? He was in his late twenties and she was in her early thirties.

Not surprisingly, Mike grew cagey in the face of Lindsay's directness. He loved her and he wanted to marry her, but why did it have to happen right now? He felt overwhelmed. Lindsay knew Mike well enough to give him his space. So with the help of friends and many a beer, he got over his fears. And by the time they got engaged, Mike was so gung ho about marriage and becoming a dad that he bought a crib.

But Lindsay wasn't even pregnant. And what was he thinking, buying a crib? Now it was *her* turn to freak out. She had said that she wanted kids, but was that really what she wanted? Suddenly she wasn't so sure. Besides, she had never backpacked across Europe. Or lived in New York City. Or dated a musician. Lindsay was having a full-blown panic attack. Meanwhile, her engagement ring was being sized, so she had started to feel like the engagement had been a figment of her imagination. Of course, that wasn't true. The proof was just sitting in the back room of a jewelry shop.

Once Lindsay began to feel a smidge saner, she decided that the best way to combat her feelings of doubt was to write a list of her fears, however absurd they were. Once she had done that, they didn't seem so frightening. Then she sat Mike down and explained to him that she was having cold feet. She knew that she loved him, but she was scared. Together they decided to put the baby talk on hold and just focus on each other. Lindsay breathed a sigh of relief. It was all she needed to know that everything was going to be okay.

Pilar

Pilar had never wanted to be one of those girls who give their boyfriends ultimatums. It wasn't her style. She felt confident it would happen, she just wasn't sure when. And whenever she'd start to feel anxious, she'd do her best to put those unprogressive "pining for a diamond" thoughts out of her head and instead try to enjoy her time with Tony.

Eventually, after five years of living together, they got engaged (she caved and had the dreaded "where are we going with this?" talk). So the last thing that Pilar expected was to find herself having concerns about their future. It wasn't like they didn't know each other. But there it was, while she was on line to buy parasols for their wedding guests: her mini freak-out.

She was standing at the checkout when she started to feel her chest getting tighter. The next thing she knew she was having trouble breathing. So she sat down, put her head between her knees, and tried to understand where all of this was coming from. And the one thing that she kept coming back to over and over was . . . her overbearing mother-in-law. Her mother-in-law had started out being genuinely helpful, in a hands-off kind of way. But as the wedding day approached, her mother-in-law was having private consultations with the photographer, calling the caterer with recipe suggestions, and faxing the DJ a list of her favorite songs. Her songs? Who gave a shit

Jessica Kaminsky

about her songs? What about Pilar and Tony's favorite songs? This woman was a like a category-four hurricane. She could not be stopped. And then, while on line for parasols that her mother-in-law was insisting she buy, she started to make sense of much of her fiancé's behavior: how he shut down in the face of conflict, how he sat back and let people do things for him, how he could be so passive at times. And Pilar thought to herself, *Is this what I want for myself? I love Tony, but I'm not going to be his mother. Oh God, is he looking for another mother? Is that why he chose me?* So she decided to seek out her best friend (and maid of honor) for advice. Later, over cocktails, Pilar aired all of her worst fears. At this point, they were just weeks away from the wedding and while she didn't really consider calling it off, there was a moment when she thought there was no way they were going to last. But her best friend assured her that she and Tony were great together, and once the wedding was over, they could push the mother-in-law out of the picture. Then, when it was finally just the two of them, they'd have an opportunity to create their own traditions without the presence of Hurricane Lorraine. Pilar's best friend assured her that in the meantime she'd step in and take care of Mom. Just hearing this, Pilar felt like a giant weight had been lifted. Never underestimate the power of a pushy mother-in-law to rock the foundation of a seemingly solid relationship.

Tips for getting through that unexpected meltdown

✳ Make a list of your fears concerning your impending nuptials, from the biggest (you don't want to lose your identity once you get married, for example) to the smallest (will he ever remember to *not* put his wet towel on the bed?). Now that you have the list, how do you feel? A little better? See, even your worst fears don't look so bad on paper. I mean, it's not like you killed a man. Unless of course you did kill a man, in which case you probably don't feel better.

✳ Do not forget to talk to your guy. He's your friend and ally in this. And chances are he knows exactly what you're going through. Remember, he was there at one point too. Need I remind you that this is the man who once tried to claim that "marriage is just a slip of paper"?

Jessica Kaminsky

✳ Between planning the wedding and sifting through your feelings, you have a lot on your plate. So on top of everything else, why put yourself in emotional exile? If you don't feel comfortable talking to your fiancé, then at least talk to someone else. A therapist. Another married couple. Your mother. Your favorite waiter. Anyone, really. Just don't bottle up how you're feeling. That's an order.

Straight from the Horse's Mouth

And now we turn to Noah, whose lady had a serious case of the pre-wedding jitters. Here's how he handled it.

When your lady first came to you and shared her feelings of doubt, how did you feel?

When we first started talking and she said that she was having some concerns, I thought she was referring to something to do with the wedding. Like maybe her dress wasn't going to be ready in time, or our bargain-basement photographer had flaked again. But once we really got into it, I realized she wasn't talking about the wedding, she was talking about her feelings about getting married. To me. She kept saying that it didn't have to do with me; it had to do with her. And I was trying to be supportive and understanding, but it was hard not to take it personally because she was talking about our wedding, our future. I was also having trouble figuring out the right thing to say. Did she want me to tell her that I didn't think we should get married? Or did she just want me to hold her hand and listen?

After our talk, I felt like a giant black cloud had parked itself over our house. Meanwhile, our wedding was approaching and I didn't know what to do. She had shared all of these anxieties with me (and seemed to feel genuinely better after our talk), but they left me feeling like crap. So what was I supposed to do now? We ended up going to a couples' therapist. The therapist helped her get to the root of her issues, which then brought up new issues for me (like how her doubts had affected my confidence in the relationship). And then after many hours and many dollars, we came to a new place of understanding. She had always had this mental image of the kind of wedding she wanted, but somehow everything falling into place had called all of that into question. Suddenly she felt predictable and out of touch with herself, while I felt completely blindsided by her confession, which then gave way to anger and uncertainty. In the end, we worked through all of our issues. We got married and I'm happy to say there are no regrets. And this time, I can say that I speak for both of us.

He Said/She Said

A real-life couple shares what brought them together and made it work.

Claire & Robbie

They started dating in early 2000 and were engaged three years later. This is their story.

She said: Robbie was the complete opposite of the kind of guy Claire usually dated. She tended to go for the emotionally absent skater punk, the aloof model, or the nerdy Jewish boy. Of course, these guys had been total disappointments. They were by turns self-involved, preoccupied, or nursing a giant drug habit. So when Claire broke up with her most recent boyfriend, she decided to go against type and agreed to be set up.

All she knew was that her date's name was Robbie. He had strawberry blond hair and hailed from the Midwest. He loved red meat and hated germs. And like her, he'd gladly spend his Saturday afternoon watching a *Real World* marathon.

He said: Before Robbie started seeing Claire, he had been in a series of relationships that had been punctuated by episodes of high drama and passive-aggressive mind games. So when he met Claire, one of the first things he noticed was how smart, reasonable, and levelheaded she seemed. She said what she meant. She didn't play games. She had a great sense of humor. She was vivacious, opinionated, and a real fox. She was completely different from any girl he had gone out with. He was in.

ACT ONE

Before the Rock

It didn't take Claire long to realize that Robbie was a cut above the guys she had dated in the past. He was funny. He was honest. He was reliable. And oh, those freckles. She didn't even know she had a thing for freckles. Before it had all been about pale, moody boys and their guitars. What the hell was happening? Was this love?

Since many of her past relationships had stalled out somewhere in the first month or two, Robbie was her first real boyfriend. At last, Claire was experiencing what it was like to be secure enough in a relationship to make plans. Future plans. Whether it was tickets to the Hollywood Bowl or Passover at her parents' place, she knew she could rely on Robbie to be by her side. Once she got comfortable with this idea, she realized she had years of unused, never-executed romantic plans, and she was determined to do them all with Robbie. One weekend, they might spontaneously check into a hotel for the night. Another weekend they could drive up the coast in search of the perfect burrito.

After two years of dating, Robbie asked Claire to move in with him. She agreed. And so Claire said good-bye to her one-bedroom bachelorette pad in West Hollywood and moved into Robbie's house in the Hollywood Hills.

He said: Before they seriously considered marriage, Robbie needed to know that he and Claire could successfully cohabitate. For him, there was a huge difference

153

between simply spending the night at someone's house and living with them. Spending the night meant that if you got in a fight or if you were in a bad mood, you could just pack up and leave. But living together, that was the real compatibility test. It meant that Claire was no longer a guest, or just spending the weekend. They were *living together*. And if they could make this work, then they could get through anything.

She said: Claire distinctly remembers the moment she knew that she was going to spend the rest of her life with Robbie. It was a cold winter night and they were getting ready for bed. Claire was doing her usual layering up. It didn't matter whether she wore socks or a sweater to bed, she was always cold. Cold hands, cold feet, cold body. So after washing her face and brushing her teeth, she came into their bedroom to find Robbie warming up her side of the bed with a hairdryer. Right then, she felt her heart swell, seeing Robbie stooped over the bed, hairdryer in hand. She knew she had a keeper.

He said: For Robbie, it took one drunken evening, which involved many shots of tequila and a break-

Jessica Kaminsky

dancing challenge, for him to realize that he was going to spend the rest of his life with Claire. Robbie had always been a little reserved when it came to expressing his emotions, playing his cards close to the vest. So he was surprised by his friend Charley's response when he told him that he knew he was going to marry Claire. Charley just turned and laughed. It had been obvious to everyone from the moment Robbie started dating Claire that he was going to marry her. Later that night, as Claire drove her gentle drunk home, he told her that he had dated a lot of girls and a lot of idiots and she was "the best of the non-idiots." Ah, love.

ACT TWO
The Proposal

She said: Claire was not expecting to get engaged any time soon. Sure, she and Robbie had looked at rings one sleepy Saturday. But she viewed the experience more as a delaying tactic on Robbie's part than actual progress. A few months earlier, when Claire had first brought up the idea of marriage, Robbie had acted, well . . . badly. He told her that he needed to be further along in his career before he could even consider getting married.

THE TRUTH BEHIND THE ROCK

Claire felt frustrated. What the hell did that mean? And how could she even compete with such an ambiguous goal? He was obviously making excuses.

He said: What Claire did not know was that Robbie had already begun to plan their engagement. While she thought he was skirting the issue entirely, Robbie was booking a hotel, making dinner reservations, and coming up with an airtight story to throw Claire off the scent.

She said: All that Claire knew about that night was that she was supposed to meet Robbie to go to his office holiday party. She wasn't looking forward to it and had tried repeatedly to get out of it. But Robbie wasn't going to let her off the hook. She had dragged him to her office Christmas party, so she knew there was no backing out. On the plus side, the party was being held at her favorite hotel. And she figured at the very least they could sneak off and have a cocktail by the pool.

He said: Robbie arrived early and put up a fake sign for his office party. When Claire arrived late she didn't think to question why the sign was written in Robbie's handwriting. As Robbie patiently waited for

Jessica Kaminsky

Claire to arrive, he started to feel genuinely nervous. However, he was pretty certain that Claire didn't suspect a thing. He had done a good job of covering his tracks. Minutes before she arrived at his faux office party, Robbie had handed his camera to a total stranger at the bar, instructing him to photograph Claire's reaction when Robbie proposed.

ACT THREE
After the Rock

She said: After she and Robbie got engaged, Claire felt giddy, thrilled. She kept looking down at her finger, admiring her new sparkly ring. Her hand looked so pretty and feminine. She was definitely going to have to step up the number of manicures she was getting. She even surprised herself by doing the most girly of all things, practicing writing her future married name on a piece of paper. Mrs. Claire Martin. Mrs. Robbie Martin. Mrs. Martin. They all sounded good to her.

But in the days that followed, the notion of being engaged started to take on surreal proportions. It wasn't that she was having doubts about Robbie. She loved him and couldn't imagine a future without him. But all of a sudden, the reality of getting married seemed insane, and she found herself examining Robbie so closely that he almost started to feel like a stranger. Claire described it as when you say a word so many times that it starts to sound like gibberish.

He said: Post-proposal Robbie felt relieved, like a ten-ton boulder had been lifted from his shoulders. He was happy. He was beyond happy. He was elated. Now almost two years later, he still recalls the night they got engaged as one of the most amazing nights of his life. Emotional, beautiful, special—everything he hoped it would be.

THE VERDICT

Claire went back to therapy. And instead of rushing into getting married, she and Robbie gave themselves the time and space they needed to get used to the idea of a life together. Claire allowed herself to go through her feelings of ambivalence, all the while knowing that in the end she wanted to be with Robbie. She just wasn't there in her head yet. Also, their year-long engagement gave Claire and Robbie an opportunity to ask themselves the scary, serious questions, like how they would raise their children, and what their views on money were. Claire feels that people tend to avoid these questions because they are so inherently unsexy. But it is exactly how we make decisions in the face of those difficult questions that contribute to a relationship's success. And after a year, Claire knew that she and Robbie would have a beautiful future together.

Rock Talk: Let's Break It Down

✳ There is nothing wrong with you if you're feeling anxious about your impending marriage. You should be nervous; it's a big deal. In fact, there'd be something wrong with you if you weren't feeling anxious.

✳ Remember you and your fiancé are on the same side. Communicate. Share your anxieties and concerns. Chances are, he can relate and maybe even offer some advice.

✳ Don't be afraid to ask the big questions. Not everything is going to be sunshine and roses, so you want to know how the two of you will handle the inevitable roadblocks.

159

* As long as you have a case of cold feet, not cold heart, everything can be worked out.

* Having doubts or concerns? Try putting them down on paper. Maybe they won't be so scary in print.

* You don't feel up to talking to your fiancé about your doubts? Then find someone else to share your concerns with. We don't want another Runaway Bride on our hands.

SOME ENGAGING HISTORY

✳ Fourteen percent of men and women do *not* wear a wedding band.

✳ The term "spooning" was first used by the lovesick men of Wales. When an infatuated man had found the love of his life, he would carve a spoon made of wood and present it to her. If she then wore it around her neck on a ribbon, she was returning his love and they would become engaged.

✳ One of history's earliest engagement rings was given to Princess Mary, daughter of Henry VIII, by the infant Dauphin of France, son of King Francis I, in the year 1518. At the time of the engagement, Princess Mary was two years old.

✳ According to Hindu tradition, rain on your wedding is considered good luck.

THE TRUTH BEHIND THE ROCK

8

RETURNING THE ROCK

I KNOW THIS WOMAN, LET'S CALL HER JANE, WHO liked to joke that even though she could barely stand her soon-to-be-husband, there was no way she'd call off the wedding. The invitations had already been mailed, the dress had been ordered, the menu had been chosen. As far as she was concerned, it would be easier just to marry the guy and get divorced than go through the humiliation of calling off a wedding and publicly breaking her fiancé's heart. At the time, I didn't know her well enough to tell if she was kidding and actually had a great relationship with her fiancé, or if this was her way of trying to get someone— anyone—to intercede.

So Jane got married. It was a big lavish affair. She and her fiancé exchanged vows; she cried, they looked happy. And I felt relieved. Jane had probably just been experiencing some pre-wedding jitters.

Years later she would tell me that she was crying that day not because she was overwhelmed with joy but because she realized she was making the biggest mistake of her life. She ended up spending the next five years with someone she knew she didn't love, eventually working up the nerve to tell him that she wasn't happy and was filing for divorce. So explain to me how that was easier than calling off the wedding.

Now, I'm not speaking with the benefit of experience here. I never once thought about calling off my wedding. I never hesitated to send out the wedding invitations; nor did I feel a pang of doubt as I stepped into my wedding dress. I never even took my ring off in a fit of anger. That said, I have known several women who, for different reasons, got engaged and then, as the wedding preparations were under way and plans were being made, realized their mistake and ended it.

Having watched these women and what they went through, let me say that calling off an engagement is no picnic. It takes balls. Giant cast-iron balls of steel. Just try to imagine your worst breakup and multiply it by ten, then factor in all the people that need to be notified (your friends, relatives, people traveling from out of town), the deposits for various wedding-related expenditures that will be lost, the engagement gifts that may or may not need to be returned. And of course, none of this even begins to factor in the emotional damage and the inevitable years spent on a therapist's couch.

Not to mention that when it's the bride that puts the kibosh on an engagement, she is now seen as the enemy, the bad girl, the heartbreaker. She loved someone and then ripped his heart out and did a dance on it for all to witness. But that was never her intention. She didn't mean to be a source of pain. She just knew in her gut that somehow this wasn't right. And instead of going through with something she knew was wrong, she did the brave thing—she faced her flawed relationship and took responsibility for it. And yet in doing so, she felt like the worst person in the world. But while it may be painful now, she has saved herself and her former fiancé years of angst in the future. So if you think that telling your engagement story over and over again is rough, think again. Try telling the story of why you called off your engagement. Here's the story of one woman who ended it before "I do."

Sharon

Sharon is from a small town in the Midwest. By the time she was twenty-five, most of her closest friends from high school were married. And even though she was living in a big city where not a single friend of hers was even remotely close to walking down the aisle, she still felt that marital push to the altar. But she did a good job of keeping those pressures at bay and instead focusing on her job.

Then she met Pete. Pete worked in the same office. He was ten years older. He had a dog and a cool apartment. They started dating. Soon she was spending weekends at his place and only going home to check her messages and pick up the mail. Things started to move pretty quickly from that point on. Pete asked if Sharon would like to move in. She did. And not long after that, they were discussing what they would name their children and where they'd like to get married. Almost a year after she and Pete started dating, they got engaged. Sharon was twenty-six.

So Sharon and Pete started to plan their wedding. They chose a date and a location, and began the tedious process of drawing up the guest list. Somewhere in the middle of this, Sharon started to notice that whenever they'd discuss anything wedding-related, she'd feel a little panicky, a little disconnected, maybe a tad short of breath. But she chalked it up to the standard wedding jitters. After all, Pete was a great guy.

As the wedding approached (they were about seven months away) and Sharon still couldn't find the time to sit down and choose invitations, she realized that something might be wrong. Sure, she was busy. She had just been promoted and she was working intense hours. But she still managed to find the time to catch up with friends. What was keeping her from sitting down with Pete for twenty minutes to look at a stupid book of stationery samples? Yet she couldn't bring herself to do it. Nor could she buy a wedding dress, choose a band, or register for all the things they needed. Not even the thought of getting matching plates or non-chipped mugs could get her to spend an hour at Crate and Barrel. None of it.

Then one night she was talking to her best friend on the phone. Her friend expressed surprise at how

Jessica Kaminsky

calm Sharon seemed, given that the wedding was now only five months away. That's when Sharon confessed that she still hadn't tried on dresses. Her friend gasped. What was she waiting for? Sharon paused— and that's when it hit her. She was waiting for someone else. And all the delays and excuses she kept making was her subconscious sending up little red flags. It was simple: She wasn't in love with Pete. Not truly, madly, deeply. Yes, she cared for him. And she definitely did not want to hurt him. But if she was being honest, she did not see herself spending the rest of her life with him. She had gotten so swept up in the idea of what was expected of her that she had forgotten to ask herself if this was the right person for her. She was just riding the tide. Her friends back home had gotten married, so why not her? And then when she met Pete, it seemed so easy to get sucked into getting married. He was older. He knew what he wanted. Who cares that she didn't?

Sharon broke up with Pete a week later. Explaining that she wasn't in love with him was the hardest thing she had ever done, but Pete ultimately understood. His heart had been crushed, but he loved Sharon enough to respect her decision. Who could blame her? She was, after all, only twenty-six years old. And she just wasn't ready for that kind of life commitment.

Exiting Etiquette

Breaking off an engagement is never easy. Words have been spoken. Feelings have been hurt. Egos have been bruised. And there's still one pesky issue left to address: Who gets to keep the ring? Not to mention the gifts from that engagement party where you both raked in the loot—the All-Clad pots, the set of professional knives, that ice cream maker. So now that the couple has chosen to part ways, who gets to walk away with those goodies?

The gifts are easy. Etiquette dictates that if a couple breaks up, all engagement gifts should be returned with a thank-you note. But of course, not all of us can be Emily Post. So if keeping the egg poacher will be less stressful than returning it with a note, then do so. Chances are your friends are going to be more concerned with your well-being than their gift. You just have to go with what feels right.

Jessica Kaminsky

As for the ring . . . there are different schools of thought. Some believe that if the woman is the one to call off the engagement, it is her obligation to return the ring. While if it is the man's decision to end things, the woman should feel free to keep the ring. The idea being that the woman's family traditionally pays for the wedding, and the value of the engagement ring can help reimburse the family for the amount of money spent thus far on the wedding.

However, in this day and age the bride's family doesn't always pay for the wedding. The bride and groom can pay. The groom's family can chip in. A rich uncle can foot the bill. You name it. But general consensus says that if the man breaks off an engagement, it is within the woman's rights to hold on to the ring.

Usually, when an engagement ends and a relationship dissolves, things do not tie up in a neat little bow. And in some cases, people have been known to turn to the legal system in a quest for answers to the "who gets to keep the ring" debate. Most courts view an engagement ring as a conditional gift. In other words, the gift isn't final until after the wedding. "Once it is established the ring is an engagement ring, it is a conditional gift" (*Heiman v. Parish, Kansas*, 1997).

THE TRUTH BEHIND THE ROCK

But the Supreme Court of Montana (*Albinger v. Harris*, 2002) feels differently. They've rejected the conditional gift principle. They believe that an engagement ring is an unconditional gift. In other words, it doesn't matter who calls the engagement off, the woman *always* gets to keep the ring.

Of course, none of this factors in the emotional cost of breaking things off with your fiancé, which is why it's important to remember that as much as it hurts now, ending a relationship that you have mixed emotions about is always for the best.

Straight from the Horse's Mouth

The good news is that the invitations had not gone out. The bad news is that Brian's fiancée wasn't just having a case of cold feet: She was calling the engagement off and leaving him.

How did she tell you she didn't want to marry you? Did you get the ring back? And what are your plans for the future?

My fiancée had gone away on business. I was expecting to pick her up from the airport in two days. Instead I got

Jessica Kaminsky

a phone call from her saying that she wasn't coming home and that she was breaking off the engagement. I was pretty much in shock when she told me. She was crying when she called. She sounded awful—sad, full of regret. Truthfully, I can't remember how I responded. I think I was just utterly speechless. As for the ring . . . she returned it to her parents, who then drove it to my folks' house, and my folks, in turn, gave it back to me. Like I really wanted it back. Currently, the ring lives in my top drawer, nestled between some old socks and a pair of boxers. When I'm ready, I plan to just sell the damn thing and try to get some money back. But for now it all feels too fresh.

My mom keeps telling me that everything is going to be fine and that my ex-fiancée saved me a lot of pain and suffering by breaking up with me now as opposed to later. Intellectually, I understand the wisdom of this statement. But right now, it's hard not to feel bitter and depressed. On the plus side, though, I used to have a beer gut. But not anymore. Turns out, depression is great for the waistline. At least I have that to thank my ex-fiancée for.

SOME ENGAGING HISTORY

✳ In 2004, actress Kim Basinger sold her 3.7-carat
Tiffany diamond engagement ring from ex-husband
Alec Baldwin at auction for $59,750. All proceeds
were donated to an animal rights charity.

✳ What became of JLo's pink diamond ring from Harry
Winston (reportedly worth 1.2 million dollars)?
According to sources, the 6.1-carat pink diamond has
been "reacquired" by Harry Winston and is back on
the market for an undisclosed sum. But don't think
you can just waltz into Harry Winston and try it on.
The ring is only available to "serious bidders."

✳ What happens to "used" diamonds? Diamonds are
sold, traded in, and reset all the time. However, no
one advertises them as "used" diamonds. They are
considered "vintage" or "estate stones." True, new
diamonds are being mined all the time, but there are
also plenty of diamonds that are recirculating. It's not
like buying a used car. A diamond does not wear out.

Jessica Kaminsky

"Amid the pine tree windbreaks and foamy
Pacific shore, Sea Ranch, California, is a
wonderful place to be dumped. The wild lilac
and ill-tempered sea lions—they'll distract your
attention for at least a few minutes after the
woman of your dreams leaves you at the altar.
That, and a hell of a lot of booze."
—An excerpt from Franz Wisner's
Honeymoon with My Brother: A Memoir
(St. Martin's Press, 2005)

He Said/She Said

A real-life couple shares what brought them together
and what tore them apart.

Introducing the now defunct . . .

Bill & Mary

They met in the winter of 2002 and broke up a year
and a half later. This is their story.

THE TRUTH BEHIND THE ROCK

ACT ONE

Tired of Dating

Bill met Mary through mutual friends. They shared the same religious faith, a passion for hiking, and a mutual desire for a big family.

He said: After their first date, Bill felt certain that Mary was the woman he wanted to marry. He was in his early thirties and he was sick of dating. So when he and Mary connected so beautifully during that initial encounter, he took it as a sign that they were meant to be together. Plus it didn't hurt that she was beautiful, passionate, and loving. Bill had never been one of those touchy-feely kinds of guys, but with Mary, it was different; they could barely keep their hands off each other. Bill hated to be away from her for even a day. Things were moving quickly, and after only a few weeks they were discussing marriage. A few months after that, they were shopping for rings.

Bill has always viewed the act of ring shopping as a metaphor for how a couple can communicate and navigate those murky waters of conflict and compromise. How a couple conducts itself while shopping for diamonds presents a small taste for how they might handle future decisions, ranging from the purchase of a home to raising children. So when he and Mary went to try on rings, he was more than relieved to see how beautifully they communicated with each other. There were no fights, no misunderstandings, no tense words. Their banter was light and playful. Plus Mary knew what she wanted—a solitaire diamond in a traditional Tiffany setting. But she was sensitive to his budget and repeatedly told him that she would be happy with whatever he got her. As far as he could tell, they had a bright future together.

Bill bought the engagement ring about a month after their trip to the jewelers and then spent the next month planning when and how he was going to propose. He even made a secret trip to visit her parents in Bethesda, Maryland, to ask for her father's permission. It was an old-fashioned thing to do—and one that he didn't necessarily agree with—but he wanted to earn her parents' confidence. And he knew that Mary would appreciate the gesture.

ACT TWO

Will You . . .

Bill proposed to Mary on his thirty-first birthday, which was a great way to surprise her. Who would ever expect to be proposed to on *someone else's* birthday? It's the perfect way to throw someone off the scent.

He said: Bill remembers the night he proposed with crystal clarity. He was feeling nervous but energized. "Baker Street" by Gerry Rafferty was playing on the radio as he drove over to Mary's house. When he arrived, she jumped in the car, a wrapped gift in her hand. She assumed they were heading out to a romantic dinner to celebrate his birthday, not suspecting for a second that they were about to get engaged. Bill told her that they had some time to kill before their reservation and suggested a walk along the promenade, a place where Mary liked to jog in the morning. She still didn't suspect a thing. He then tucked a bottle of champagne in his bulky jacket, making sure to keep Mary on the opposite side of the booze. After walking for a few minutes, Bill suggested they sit down and enjoy the view. Mary obliged, and that's when he proposed. He kept it short and simple. He didn't get down on one knee. He simply held her hand, told her that he loved her, and asked if she would marry him. She kissed him and said yes. Then they drank the bottle of champagne and toasted their future life together. Bill went to bed that night a happy man . . . but it wouldn't last.

ACT THREE
What Have I Done?

The freak-out started the moment he opened his eyes and turned to see Mary sleeping by his side. *What the hell have I done?* he remembers thinking. Sure, they had amazing chemistry and she was the most beautiful woman he had ever seen. But how could he pin a future on sexual attraction and good looks? He needed more. He suddenly found himself craving an intellectual connection, one that he and Mary had never shared. He grew critical of her. She wasn't a reader the way he was. Yes, she read the newspaper, but had he ever seen her pick up a book for fun? Never. As Bill lay in bed, he started to compile a list of all of his buddies who were

THE TRUTH BEHIND THE ROCK

married. They had friendships with their mates—deep, lifelong, spiritually and intellectually challenging relationships. He just didn't think he could go that deep with Mary. It wasn't going to work. He needed to get out. And all of these feelings had welled up in him the morning after their engagement, before she was even awake.

When he finally shared some of his concerns with Mary, she was understandably hurt, but she was committed to making changes. She wanted to show him that they could be more than lovers. They could be friends and they could be emotional partners, and it was a journey she was willing to make with him. Bill could see that Mary was hurting, so he tried to put his doubts aside and together they began to plan the wedding. They set the date, chose a location, and ordered the invitations. Things were moving along. But a pall had been cast over their engagement and Bill felt Mary pulling away. One day she came back from the hairdresser sobbing. Pachelbel's "Canon in D" had been playing in the background. It was the song that she always imagined she'd one day walk down the aisle to, and yet here she was engaged and

Jessica Kaminsky

miserable. She wasn't a blushing bride-to-be. She was depressed and she knew in her heart that something wasn't right. At that point, Bill knew it was over. The writing was on the wall.

First, Mary asked Bill to return the keys to her apartment. Then she slowly started carting her belongings home from his place—her favorite soap that she kept in the medicine chest, her pajamas, a few blouses in the closet. And then one day she took the ring off and handed it to Bill. At the time, Bill said some hurtful things to Mary. But he really couldn't blame her for breaking off their engagement. He had been cruel, making her try to prove her worth to him. As he walked away from her house for the last time, he was already filled with regret.

WHAT ABOUT THE RING?

A friend suggested Bill post it on eBay, but somehow the idea of people casually bidding on the ring that he had so carefully chosen didn't sit well with him. The ring deserved a better fate. He toyed with the dramatic act of tossing it into the ocean, but that seemed wasteful. He then thought about giving it to a family member, but what would that accomplish? He even considered framing it and hanging it on his wall as an example of his stupidity. But out of all the options that ran through his mind, there was one thing he knew that he could never do— he couldn't give the ring to another woman. That diamond had been spoiled, tainted, polluted by failed love.

In the end, Bill ended up returning the ring to a jeweler. Not to the jeweler who had originally sold him the ring, but to another jewelry dealer, many states away, who specialized in the "redistribution of secondhand rings." As Bill watched the dealer strip the diamond of its setting and place it on a velvet pad to examine it, he felt a tug of sadness. By letting go of the ring, he realized that even though he hadn't seen her in close to a year, he was finally saying good-bye to Mary.

Jessica Kaminsky

Rock Talk: Let's Break It Down

✳ The embarrassment of calling off a wedding is nothing compared to the angst and pain of staying in a loveless marriage, so do yourself a favor and have that difficult talk with your fiancé.

✳ No matter what you think, getting married, then divorced is not easier than calling off a wedding.

✳ You end it, you return it. Baby does not get to keep the bling when she breaks his heart.

✳ If you're putting off sending out those invitations, there may be a reason.

✳ Crying all the time? Can't sleep at night? Drinking excessively? It's time to take a look at your behavior and ask yourself why you are acting this way—it may be that you're with the wrong guy.

THE ROCK REVIEW

ONE OF THE REASONS I FELT COMPELLED TO WRITE this book was to dispel the myth of the perfect engagement. This is not to say that your guy is incapable of surprising you with a ring when you least suspect it. Because he is. And if he's smart, he will. It's more to show that the actual engagement can be the final leg of a long, long, *long* journey. A journey on which you've had to endure many gut-wrenching conversations, unspoken frustrations, tense negotiations, and last-ditch ultimatums.

When women discuss getting engaged, rarely do they lead off with an anecdote about their fiancé's apprehension about marriage. *Funny story: One night, my boyfriend of three years told me that he didn't believe in marriage. Isn't that hilarious?* Instead women tend to go through the anxiety-inducing, angst-ridden pre-engagement talks by themselves, silently wishing that their boyfriend could be more like their friend's fiancé. Meanwhile, unbeknownst to them, that same friend (you know, the one with the "perfect" engagement) had to overcome obstacles of her own, like . . . warming up her then-boyfriend to the idea of marriage while trying not to take his lack of enthusiasm personally.

My point is that everyone has their own issues—whether it's a boyfriend who has shut down ever since the subject of marriage was first mentioned, or a friend's recent engagement that has suddenly caused you to covet something you never thought twice about before. Little things, small events, tiny comments seep into our subconscious, and it's tough not to be affected by the progress of others. Which is why it's important to remember that we all do things at different times and on different schedules. And just because your guy is dragging his heels or gets visibly shifty any time someone mentions their upcoming nuptials doesn't mean that he won't come around. Give him the time and space he needs to get used to the idea.

The one thing that is essential during this period of pre-engagement purgatory is to be honest about your needs and communicate them to your partner. Men are not mind readers—if you want to get engaged, you need to bring up the subject. Of course, bringing up your desire to get engaged is not an easy task. And there are times when you might explode out of frustration. If this happens, and it could, you are not detracting from the romance of his eventual proposal. Just because you spoke to your guy and clued him in to how you're feeling and even urged him on by saying that you'd like to get engaged sooner rather than later does not make your engagement any less special or unique.

As much as I wish that Dave had been able to stare into a crystal ball and know that I wanted to get engaged, I also fully recognize that I wanted something from him and therefore I needed to sit down and have that talk with him. But it took time. For a while I refused to have that conversation with him and instead I traipsed around our house getting annoyed at the smallest thing and rolling my eyes. And while Dave certainly could tell that something was upsetting me due to my beleaguered sighs and general irritability, he might just as easily have thought I'd had a rough day at work. So I had no choice but to tell him what was on my mind (the state of our relationship) and what I wanted from him (to get engaged). Looking back, I wish that I had been maybe a bit calmer and shed a few less tears, but my feelings on the matter had to be voiced in order for us to continue having a communicative relationship. If you want something, you need to express yourself. So if you take nothing else from this book, remember to talk, share, yell, shout, get messy, say things you regret, and speak your mind. It's when we bottle feelings up and turn inward that we go insane.

Look, I got lucky. I have an amazing guy. But it took us a long time to be able to talk seriously (and calmly) about marriage—our expectations, his lack of interest, my growing impatience at his lack of interest, et cetera. When it came down to it, Dave found the idea of marriage conventional and unnecessary, while I saw it as an essential step toward spending our lives together. Over time and many heated discussions, we found a middle ground. Or maybe Dave came around to my way of seeing things. But more likely, I just wore him down. However it happened, Dave eventually became comfortable with the idea of marriage and not long after, we got engaged. So while there are no guarantees for our future, I have no regrets. I'm glad we had those painfully frank, often tear-inducing discussions. I know now that we are a stronger couple for them.

So whether or not you want to get engaged, already are engaged, or have a friend who has been feeling that tug toward the altar, take comfort in knowing that no matter how it all unfolds (be it loud, loving, or somewhere in between), you are not the first person to get fed up and issue an ultimatum. And that's okay. You're entitled to want to get engaged. Just try your best to be patient and hear your boyfriend out, and have a smidge of faith that if it was meant to be, it'll happen. In the meantime, talk to your friends, swap stories, voice your frustrations, and communicate. There's no reason to go through it alone.

Straight from the Horse's Mouth

Every once in a while it would be nice to understand what is going on inside that brain of his. Eric shares some male insight on the subject of engagements.

What advice do you have for women who want to get engaged but find themselves increasingly frustrated by their boyfriend's lack of momentum?

I guess, try to be aware that guys process information differently than women do. And just because he isn't ready to propose doesn't mean his feelings for you aren't real. Remember, patience is a virtue. So give your guy a chance to come around. Let him decide that he wants to get married, and not that he has to get married.

I have a theory. It's a little controversial. But based on my own experience, I believe that sometimes you have to hate someone before you can really learn to love them. Let me explain. In the beginning of a relationship, it's easy to be in love. You're just getting to know someone. You're having sex all the time. You're happy. You never fight. The world is your oyster. But inevitably the honeymoon period ends and things get more challenging. Couples fight and tensions rise. And many people find themselves completely floored by these new developments. What happened to their old relationship? They become disillusioned, fall out of love, and break up.

But I feel that if you stick it out through the fights (you learn how to love the person you can't stand), then you can make it through anything. Once you've had the disagreements about finances, family, and commitment, your relationship will be stronger and this will help you learn how to better communicate with each other down the line.

SOME ENGAGING HISTORY

✳ Brides wear "something old" on their wedding day in order to create continuity with the past.

✳ Approximately seven thousand couples get married every day in the United States.

✳ New Year's Day and Valentine's Day are the two most popular days to get married in Las Vegas.

✳ Seventeen tons of gold are used each year to make wedding rings in the United States.

Jessica Kaminsky

He Said/She Said

It didn't seem fair that I got to tell my side of the story without ever letting you hear Dave's version. So here it is . . .

Jessica & Dave

We met in the fall of 1997, shared our first illicit kiss on New Year's Eve, and started dating a few weeks later. We got engaged, after five years of dating, on . . . you guessed it, New Year's Eve. This is Dave's side of the story.

ACT ONE

Never Leave Your Lady Unattended on New Year's Eve

He said: When Jessica and I first met, she was dating someone else. But as far as I could tell, it was the tail end of a dying relationship. Still, we were just friends who liked to occasionally hang out and drink too much. Then one night I bumped into her at a club. We hadn't seen each other in a while. But when I spotted her across the room I got that butterflies-in-the-stomach feeling. In that split second, I knew everything had changed. I had a crush on Jessica.

A few weeks later I went over to her house for a New Year's Eve barbecue. Her boyfriend at the time was getting ready to go home for the night and I couldn't help but wonder, *What guy leaves his lady alone on New Year's Eve?* But I wasn't going to say anything. It was his loss, right? Besides, with her boyfriend out of the picture, I was free to flirt. So after he split, I moved his plate away, scooted next to her, and spent the next three hours by her side. Then, at midnight, I took a chance and kissed her on the lips. It was pretty amazing. I'm guessing she felt the same way, because the next week, she broke up with that other guy and never looked back. That was eight years ago.

For our first date, I took her to a small Italian restaurant. We sat on the outdoor patio and drank giant glasses of wine. Everything was going really well. Conversation was flowing, until the waiter came to take our order and I asked for the house salad. Based on her reaction (shock with a sprinkle of disgust), you would have thought that I had just done something really embarrassing, like farting loudly. I remember she just kind of stared at me like, *Oh, no. What's wrong with this guy? Does he not eat? Is he on a diet? Does he hate food?!* Of course, I could have cleared up the whole matter on the spot, but it seemed a little early to be declaring my feelings of love (okay, lust) for someone. So instead of saying the reason I didn't order my usual tub of pasta was because I was nervous I might be falling in love, I just let her think I was a picky eater and hoped that she'd look beyond the salad incident and let me take her out on a second date.

ACT TWO
This Feels Nice

He said: Unlike my other relationships, which had required constant work, Jessica and I had an immediate connection. Maybe it was because we had both come out of fight-filled relationships, but ours had an ease to it that was new to me. Our relationship felt effortless. Not that it didn't require maintenance or attention. It just didn't need the kind of work that makes you sigh, shake your head, and wish that you had dated your girlfriend's best friend instead. With Jessica I never had to worry whether or not she was mad at me. Because if she was mad, she'd tell me. Jessica didn't play games. She didn't use Jedi mind tricks to manipulate a situation.

So while I never had one of those single, revelatory moments wherein I realized that I wanted to spend the rest of my life with her, I knew that after spending an entire weekend together, I didn't want to leave. And as far as I could tell, that was a pretty good sign.

ACT THREE
A Rude Awakening

He said: Because we didn't have a high drama kind of relationship, punctuated by breakups and threats of breaking up, it wasn't until Jessica voiced her desire to get engaged that we experienced our first rough patch. We had just moved in together and had been dating for close to three years. We loved each other and felt comfortable making plans for our future, and yet when she first brought up the subject of marriage, I was surprised by my visceral anti-engagement response. I felt like we didn't need to rock the boat. Things seemed to be going perfectly fine to me, so why make such a big fuss? Besides, historically I've always had a healthy distrust of most institutions and traditions. And I refused to get married just because that's what we were supposed to do. But really, the truth was that weddings made me nervous. I'm a private person and the thought

Jessica Kaminsky

of getting up in front of a lot of people and saying intimate things to my lady, well . . . it just wasn't my idea of a good time. Also, marriage had never particularly interested me. Not because I didn't want to share my life with someone. I did. And that person was Jessica. I simply never felt like I needed a certificate to do it.

THE VERDICT

After many difficult conversations, I agreed to get engaged, but I told Jessica that I needed to give myself a year to get everything in order. A year sounded reasonable to her, and so she relaxed and gave me the space I needed to do my thing. So a year to the day later, we got engaged.

We've been married for close to two years now and I can say with confidence that I love being married. It makes things easier on a practical level and lets us put aside questions about "the future" and concentrate on other things, like whether or not we can afford to buy a flat-screen TV. Plus, after we got engaged, I noticed a tangible shift in Jessica's behavior. She seemed a lot happier and more relaxed. We argued less. Overall, marriage suits us even if the road getting there was sometimes rocky.

WHAT ABOUT THE RING?

I was lucky enough to have a friend of the family who was in the jewelry business to help me out. Which is a good thing because I'm the kind of guy who needed "a guy" to walk me through the shopping process. As for the ring . . . Jessica gave me some pretty unambiguous guidelines in the form of a torn-out Tiffany advertisement, and if that weren't clear enough, her best friend was recruited to help provide counsel. But really her friend was there to steer me in the right direction and help me circumvent my own bad instincts.

Rock Talk: Let's Break It Down

✴ Explain to me what a perfect engagement is. Now forget it. Do yourself a favor and don't get hung up on perfect.

✴ Don't be afraid to share your tales of frustration with your friend. Chances are, she may have a story or two to toss into the mix.

✴ Tap into your inner Dalai Lama and try to find a sense of patience and calm.

* Who cares about other people's progress? Focus on your own.

* Gut-wrenching conversations? Unspoken frustrations? Tense negotiations? Sounds familiar to me. As far as I can tell, you must be doing something right.

* Whatever you do, don't hold it in. Be honest with your guy. Let him know how you're feeling and that you want to get engaged.

* Okay, you got upset and lost your cool. So what? It doesn't have to take away from the romance of your eventual engagement.

* Instead of thinking of it as you versus him, remember you're on the same team, even if you see things differently.

THE TRUTH BEHIND THE ROCK

ACKNOWLEDGMENTS

THERE ARE SO MANY PEOPLE TO THANK. FIRST off, I want to thank my friend and editor, Trish Boczkowski, for encouraging me to write this book way back when I was hideously pregnant, housebound, and looking for something to do. I'd also like to thank Amanda Lasher and Rebecca Paley for providing endless amounts of support and insight throughout the writing of this book in the form of notes on half-written sections, and words of encouragement during those tough chapters, of which there were many. And to Olivia Booth, Jocelyn Morse, and Kristen Muller, whose friendship and candid advice was crucial during my writing. Also, I'm forever indebted to the ladies of the Cone: Gigi McCreery, Linda Mathious, Heather MacGillvray, Sky Kunerth, and again Amanda, for their friendship, their ability to listen, their solid advice on both writing and relationships, and for just being . . . fantastic ladies. And then there are all the people who let me interview them, who willingly shared the evolution of their relationships—their funny stories, their frustrating tales, their vulnerable moments, their regrettable behavior, and their satisfying conclusions . . . I am truly grateful for their stories. This book would be nothing without them. Now, as much as I'd love to thank each person, I did promise to change all names to protect the innocent. So you know who you are and, again, thank you. I'd also like to give a big thank-you to my agents, Brian Lipson and Lisa Harrison, at Endeavor. And finally an extra-special thank-you to my two men, my two Rocks, one small and one tall . . . Orson and Dave. I love you.

Jessica Kaminsky